A CULTURE OF VALUES

The Principles of
Transformational Leadership

LAURA THOMPSON

morehouse PUBLISHING

Morehouse Publishing
19 East 34th Street
New York, NY 10016
www.churchpublishing.org

Morehouse Publishing is an imprint of Church Publishing Incorporated.

Cover design by David Baldeosingh Rotstein
Typeset by Westchester Publishing Services

ISBN 978-1-64065-817-2 (hardcover)
ISBN 978-1-64065-818-9 (eBook)

Library of Congress Control Number: 2025946807

For You

POINT OF VIEW

This book is a reflection on what I've observed,
past and present.
Some ideas and strategies may resonate;
others may not.
There are a plethora of frameworks.
I've cited those that have resonated with my clients.
Adopt what's useful.
Let go of what doesn't work.

I invite you to
start with a beginner's mind,
question what's true and what's not,
delve deeper toward self-awareness,
and be open.

You're on a lifelong journey,
personally and professionally.
May you become the best version of yourself!

TABLE OF CONTENTS

PART ONE

A HOLISTIC FOUNDATION

INTRODUCTION

AUTHENTIC LEADERSHIP

IDEALS, MINDFULNESS,
AND COMPASSION

Tell me, what is it you plan to do with your one wild and precious life?
—Pulitzer Prize–winning poet Mary Oliver

Leadership today is more demanding than ever. The rapid pace of change, evolving workplace dynamics, and the pressure to deliver results create a daunting challenge: How do you remain true to yourself and your values while guiding your team through uncertainty? Your leadership doesn't just influence productivity and outcomes—it shapes the culture, morale, and overall well-being of those around you, including yourself.

The consequences of inauthentic leadership are profound. When leaders operate without self-awareness or fail to connect with their teams, trust erodes, motivation wanes, and turnover spikes. Beyond the workplace, the ripple effects extend into personal relationships and broader organizational culture. When leaders ground themselves in authenticity, embracing self-awareness, mindfulness, and compassion, they cultivate an environment where both people and performance thrive.

Over the past three decades, I've worked with leaders across various industries around the globe who confront these challenges. My approach in working with them is deeply rooted in values-driven leadership, informed by my journey from a traditional Christian upbringing to an exploration of Buddhist teachings. This shift broadened my perspective, offering insights into conscious, intentional leadership that prioritizes introspection, presence, mindfulness, empathy, compassion, and ethical decision-making.

In this book, I'll share these insights with you and offer practical, actionable strategies that will help you cultivate a leadership style that is both effective and deeply aligned with your core beliefs. This approach will help you strengthen yourself through personal mastery, which you can then pay forward to your team, organization, and beyond to society. Implementing these strategies will also create a more balanced, integrated, and fulfilling life.

LEADERSHIP IN ACTION: A CASE STUDY

Let me share a real-world example. In brief, Dallas, a team leader whom I coached, was grappling with his team's low morale and high turnover in the IT & Engineering Division at a Fortune 100 telecommunications company. His team was frustrated and disengaged because of a recent reorganization with layoffs. Through our work together, I introduced him to values-based leadership and mindful communication practices that helped him become aware of his colleagues' needs and be more attuned to their perspectives. As he began to actively listen on a deeper level and respond with empathy, the dynamics within his team shifted. Trust was rebuilt. Collaboration improved. His team members felt understood, valued, and respected. Together they established their core values and created a vision and mission in alignment with the team's and company's goals. Their mission statement became . . . *to serve and lead our peers so that they're empowered to be successful.* The mission derived from the team's values-based premise: *What fulfills us is being of service to our team and our customers.*

The consequence of this exercise was transformative. Dallas witnessed improved team morale and retention as well as increased positive interactions with the team's key corporate stakeholders. The impact didn't stop there. Inspired by the transformation at work, Dallas brought these practices into his personal life, applying mindful listening and values-based engagement with his wife and teenage daughter. The result? Stronger connections, more meaningful conversations, and a newfound sense of harmony both at home and in his broader social circles.

His story underscores a vital truth: When you lead with authenticity, values, mindfulness, and compassion, the benefits extend far beyond the workplace, enriching every aspect of your life.

LEARN FROM EXEMPLARY LEADERS

Throughout the book, I will introduce you to leaders, some widely known, others less so, who exemplify the power of authentic leadership. Who has influenced you? It could be a family member, a mentor, a colleague, a historical figure, or a trailblazer you admire. What qualities make them stand out? What values do they embody?

A leader who profoundly shaped my understanding of values-based leadership is Nelson Mandela. I had the unexpected privilege of meeting him at Tribeca Grill in Manhattan while dining with my brother, then the CEO of a wealth management firm. Mandela was celebrating his birthday, surrounded by his entourage. I decided to approach him, to express my admiration for his extraordinary leadership. I told him I had written about him in one of my books. Mandela took my hand, held it gently, and shared a few kind words. I wished him well and returned to my seat, deeply moved by the encounter. His presence was magnetic, his humility striking.

Mandela's leadership journey was one of profound self-mastery and professional transformation. From a revolutionary fighter against apartheid to a bridge-building statesman, he led South Africa as its first democratically elected president at age seventy-five. His was a long road, requiring great patience, but he changed the narrative of domination and colonialism to one of peace and democracy. His leadership principles were grounded in forgiveness, compassion, and respect for human dignity. Despite the immense challenges he faced, he never abandoned his values, proving that true leadership isn't about power; it's about service, integrity, and the courage to create meaningful change.

Among the things that made Mandela extraordinary was his ability to make every individual feel seen. No matter the setting, he met people with full presence, respect, and authenticity. His leadership serves as a powerful reminder that when we lead with mindfulness and compassion, we create environments where people feel valued and inspired to give their best.

MOVING ON

Building upon the holistic foundation of values-based leadership, the second portion of this book emphasizes how humancentric leadership helps foster high-performing, collaborative teams. The third portion revolves around responsible leadership in the Intelligence Age at both the organizational and societal levels. As a leader, you can apply various forward-thinking strategies and implement novel concepts to thrive and rise above complexity. I then circle back to the concept of how to know yourself through personal mastery and how you can participate in building your organization's legacy as well as your own.

Finally, the book concludes with multiple reflections based on the universal themes that consistently come up in my conversations while coaching leaders. These are organized into eighteen stand-alone essays. I hope you will bounce around and read them as you see fit—in whatever order—based on your needs and curiosity. Clients have told me that they found this information valuable and applicable to both their work and their personal life. Their reflections underscore a deeper truth: Leadership growth is not a destination, but a journey that starts with intention and unfolds through practice.

Your Journey Begins Here

While leadership is the focus, the true value lies in the transformation it inspires both within you and around you. As you read, I hope you'll gain actionable insights as well as practical tools that you can put to effective use, and that the real-world examples help you refine your leadership approach. The methods I recommend throughout this book are based on years of primary research, as well as collaborations with innovative thought leaders and others at distinguished universities worldwide.

Each chapter includes exercises designed to reinforce your learning and encourage you to experiment, reflect, and grow. My goal is to equip you with the mindset and strategies to navigate challenges; build meaningful relationships; lead with authenticity, mindfulness, and purpose; and thrive amidst uncertainty and complexity.

This book is also a call to action. Leadership today demands more than competence; it requires courage, integrity, and a willingness to evolve. The world is at a crossroads. There is an urgent need for leaders who will champion social good, empower others, and create inclusive, values-driven cultures.

Are you ready to embark on this journey? To embrace curiosity, experimentation, and a growth mindset? To challenge conventional thinking and redefine what leadership means in today's world?

Let us create a movement. Let your imagination lead the way, informed by principles and strategies embraced in this book that form the oxygen of transformative leadership.

Your first step begins now.

ONE

SELF-AWARENESS, CORE VALUES, AND PURPOSEFUL LEADERSHIP

Knowing others is wisdom; knowing oneself is enlightenment.

—Lao Tzu

Why values-based leadership? Like President Nelson Mandela, most truly inspirational leaders first look within and change themselves and then go on to have a positive impact on those around them, even the world. The results of such introspection lead to evolution of oneself, others, and organizations, based on values, forgiveness, and ultimately unconditional love.

Innovative, inspirational, and transformative leaders abound across the private, public, and government sectors as well as in families, local communities, cities, states, countries, and regions around the globe. They are the pioneers, the change catalysts, the rebels that influence humankind. As pioneers and catalysts for positive change, it's not unusual to encounter active resistors and skeptics. However, those who become change warriors do so because they are comfortable with change and are agile during times of uncertainty, thus driving a current condition to a better future state.

What do such leaders have in common? Transformative leaders often take a different route from most others. They may start out like explorers with curious minds—always asking questions and thinking about how to improve programs, processes, and systems in an experimental fashion—and are solutions-focused, willing to investigate multiple iterations, sometimes even failing forward, knowing that they will learn lessons that can be applied to future situations. Robert Frost could have been describing change agents when he wrote, "Two roads diverged in a wood, and I—I took the one less traveled by, and that has made all the difference." Are you taking the road less traveled and following your unique path?

What else do many rebels with a cause have in common? Often it is sacrifice for the common good. Most of you strive for excellence in leadership. Some of you are visionary leaders who are both brave and motivated to provide better conditions for stakeholders. Not everyone is a visionary, and we need talented people to develop strategic plans and lead those who are adept at executing. Everyone has a role to play in this game.

The journey starts with self-reflection and exploration of your core values. Once you build this foundation, it becomes easier to search for what brings you meaning, fulfillment, and purpose, eventually building a legacy— whatever it may be, whether advocating for a cause, creating a family dynasty, or contributing to your community with impact. Reaching these goals entails challenging yourself to stretch beyond limiting beliefs to become the best possible version of yourself.

Imagine you are a bricklayer, think about doing it with the intention of building a monument to faith, such as a cathedral, a mosque, a temple, or simply an amazing feat of architecture. Picture the Taj Mahal, the famed mausoleum in Agra, India, commissioned in 1631 by the Mughal emperor Shah Jahan for his beloved wife, Mumtaz Mahal, who was the love of his life. Building something bigger than yourself becomes a parable about the power of purpose and a higher meaning in work and life that can bring fulfillment and love.

CONSCIOUS LIVING AND SELF-DISCOVERY

Effort, timing, and luck notwithstanding, what you have done in your past has brought you to where you are now. While psychotherapy deals with uncovering the past to heal unconscious and conscious wounds, coaching may review the past but focus on the present and how to figure out what to do next to improve your life. The conscious living and self-discovery exercise involves looking backward, presencing, and then looking forward, with the aim of gaining insight into how you as an individual can imagine a more meaningful, fulfilling, and purposeful life.

Looking backward provides the context and background for you to reflect on how you have managed both challenges and successes. *Presencing* is practiced through stillness, meditation, or prayer as a method for centering yourself to unveil your inner wisdom. Honor yourself with self-compassion and allow yourself to be grateful for your successes. In times of adversity, ask how can you reframe this challenge as a blessing? As a gift? Next, recalibrate this positive reframe into your present existence to set yourself up to move ahead with your new mindset. *Looking forward* involves imagining your future aligned with your best interests for the highest good. This process helps you to see the gifts you've gained from both your challenges and successes and is useful as a means to continually evolve and elevate.

This approach becomes even more powerful when grounded in real-life experiences like that of my client, Dr. Naomi, a Black woman who has earned the distinction of becoming a high-ranking military officer in the aviation service. We went through the conscious living and self-discovery exercise together.

By *looking backward*, she acknowledged her stellar career and felt grateful to have allies but, as a female in a male-dominated organization, she still felt isolated, lonely, and discriminated against. This is a recurring theme for women in tech, finance, aviation, and likely many other industries.

With *presencing*, she realized social injustice had increased awareness of the need for systemic change worldwide to create a feeling of greater belonging.

Looking forward helped Naomi create an internal blueprint for belonging. It included implementing crucial conversations, working to further social justice, and promoting a culture of belonging. It was not anger-based; it came from the heart, it came from unconditional love, and it motivated her to get up every morning. Naomi imagined the biggest change in her future would be systematizing her blueprint of belonging within her branch of the military through communication and collaboration, along with rallying allies, forming coalitions, and implementing policies approved by senior decision-makers. She had a plan to get boots on the ground with change agents across generations and divisions, to create systemic improvement in a culture of core values focusing on long-term sustainability. Her journey illustrates how personal purpose can create systemic leadership strategies that drive broader institutional change.

There are always golden opportunities to create better environments. As the military is still mainly a white male "club," flattening the playing field was Naomi's idea of heaven on earth, and since it is a hierarchical organization, her strategy began with the top brass. Her plan was to utilize the following steps: 1) deal with the "knowns," 2) build a culture of gender and racial equality and equity where all are welcome and feel they belong, and 3) achieve greater diversity through meritocracy above the rank of Major, that would include Black people, people of color (POC), women, and the LBGTQIA+ population.

Alongside her distinguished military leadership, Naomi serves as a chaplain, using both platforms to advance social justice and drive change within her spheres of influence. Her ultimate goal is, and it may well be her legacy, to become the second Black woman to be nominated by the president and confirmed by the Senate as a two-star major general, the highest peacetime rank in the United States Armed Forces. (She promised to invite me when it happens, and I'm backing her all the way, just as I do with all my clients.)

Near the end of our coaching engagement, Naomi affirmed, "Perfection is not the goal; growth is!" This realization liberated her by lifting the fear of making mistakes. As long as you're learning, it's not failure; it's growth. That's the power of choosing progress over perfection. My clients are blessings in my life, and our work together is a mutual evolution.

In your own unique and authentic way, you aspire to make this a better world. You have the potential to tap into your personal power and utilize resources to accelerate change, even if change and uncertainty can be both scary and exciting. Acknowledge your paradoxical emotions. Move on. Find pragmatic reasons to stretch yourself beyond your comfort zone. Create an action plan and take baby steps to implement it. Form alliances among your family, friends, and colleagues for support. Make your allies your account- ability partners. If you feel stuck, gather diverse points of view to help you uncover limiting beliefs that may be blocking you from moving toward your goals, aspirations, and dreams. Be guided by actions that have a positive impact on others in your circles of influence. Serving something greater than yourself helps you feel useful, valuable, and optimistic.

LIVE YOUR VALUES

Most people are generally aware of their beliefs and values but may not be able to state them explicitly without a bit of thought. I ask my clients to come up with their three most important values and how they unconsciously or consciously have influenced the way they led their lives. Emotions are a barometer of truth that show you when you're in sync with your values. When you are in misalignment, you can become engulfed by negative emo- tions; feel frustrated, angry, or hopeless; or even find yourself in a state of inertia. Unless you engage in conscious reflection, you may not realize what triggered those feelings. When you're in alignment with your core values, you experience high energy, joy, peace, confidence, worthiness, and integrity. You become unstoppable in leading a meaningful life.

This is a bit of a deep dive, but once you uncover your values, you can use them as guideposts to make intentional decisions that will help you take the best course of action in a variety of situations. They will also help you build better relationships and collaborate with others—your family, your team at work, your organization, and your community. This tool equips you to understand what matters most and to live authentically with purpose. As the philosopher Socrates said, "To know thyself is the beginning of wisdom."

Each person has a unique collection of values. My top three values are curiosity, being of service, and fun. Many friends, colleagues, and clients share similar values. Knowing your values helps you gain a deeper understanding of yourself. You may inherently know them, but it's an interesting exercise to state them out loud.

It is important to recognize that your values may conflict with other people's values, which can sow discord. There's no right or wrong set of values, but it's important to agree to disagree and be able to have difficult conversations based on your diverse points of view. Embracing disagreements with an open mind leads to innovative solutions and breakthroughs. Contradictory skill sets may cause disruptions, but will drive evolutionary or even revolutionary change, often pressing humankind forward in positive ways.

It doesn't matter who you are, we all have an individual set of values, although we may share the same basic ethics. Some clients have held family devotion as their primary value, followed by being a provider, and taking care of others. These values translated positively into mentoring, coaching, and developing team members professionally, but, at the same time, they had to be mindful that their devotion to family might get in the way of work. A holistic approach, whether interacting with family, managing a team, or leading an organization, is essential.

Fun fact: Did you know that human beings are more than 99 percent genetically identical? Service to others focuses on people first, valuing them as human beings, respecting them for who and what they are, and looking beyond surface differences such as color, race, religion, sexual orientation, political stance, and more. Today, a growing shift in consciousness is bringing renewed attention to our shared humanity, and with it, a deeper call to treat one another with dignity and respect. It's up to each of us to honor that truth by leading with empathy and embodying it in how we treat others, This commitment to empathy and values-driven action isn't just theoretical; it's something I actively share in my work with emerging leaders.

As a guest lecturer at California Lutheran University in Professor Tracy Nickl's class, I had the opportunity to explore these themes further when I spoke about values-based team leadership. As in any organization, a student team leader's first job is to know their own personal values, then translate them into team values, which in this case was to create a mission statement in alignment with the professor's goals regarding their team projects.

This was an engaged, interactive experience. The students came from diverse backgrounds, but *respect* turned out to be the primary value they all held in common. These are our future leaders, and it gave me hope that they are enlightened and care about making the world a better place.

In business, values tend to be quite diverse. They can include safety, status, money, structure, stability, loyalty, financial responsibility, work-life balance, fitness, nutrition, rest, service to others, meaning, connection, belonging, purpose, sustainability, transparency, honesty, clarity in communications, learning, growth, integrity, authenticity, a sense of humor, and helping others be the best version of themselves.

One of my clients, Adbul, was a deep thinker, whose core value, to serve others, was the basis of his leadership style. He built teams around sharing issues and problem-solving to create an environment of bonding, belonging, contributing, and feeling valued, heard, and acknowledged. His ongoing intention was to coach team members to be better versions of themselves both in and outside the workplace. He happily acknowledged when a team member provided a solution with a better outcome than his own and encouraged other team members to do so. In this way he helped each of them grow.

Implementing a values-based leadership style serves as both an anchor and a beacon during times of change and, today, change is constant. This model helps leaders build alliances and create meaningful connections to others. It inspires and motivates. It increases engagement through exchanging knowledge, understanding varying points of view, embracing multiculturalism, implementing gender equality and gender equity, and creating a space of belonging where everyone feels safe and accepted. Sharing your values deepens respect and trust. A values-based foundation creates an open, transparent, and harmonious environment where you and everyone else thrives. Values, forgiveness, and unconditional love are the oxygen of life and transformative leadership.

This commitment to values-driven leadership delivers measurable results. According to a 2022 Towers & Watson report, companies with engaged employees have a 19 percent increase in operating income over a 12-month period, whereas without engagement, operating income decreases by 33 percent. Hence, leveraging the value of human capital in a dignified way contributes to a significant return on investment (ROI).[1]

Unfortunately, many clients have mentioned a lack of authenticity within their organizations. The company talks about values but does not follow through on the talk. This can result in "greenwashing"—for example, when companies routinely mislead consumers that they are eco-champions. Fossil fuel companies sometimes say they are focused on low-carbon energy products when a majority of their business consists in oil and gas, which contribute to global warming. Others, such as Nestlé, Coca-Cola, and PepsiCo, proclaim that their packaging will be 100 percent recyclable or reusable; however, the *Break Free from Plastic 2020* annual report named them the world's top plastic polluters.[2]

Increasingly, employees are disturbed when companies do not walk the talk, whether related to values-based leadership, sustainability, climate crises, and other disasters. Some consider it "whitewashing" when a company does not implement a mission to live by its stated values or practices. As a values-based leader, you can be a role model by living your values for your company and teammates and colleagues as well as with friends, family, and community.

LEADING WITH PURPOSE

Consider the experience of a client I'll refer to as Alexander, a millennial professional I worked with to alter his leadership approach to align with sustainable business practices. First, we went through the personal values exercise; then I asked him to do it with his wife. He remarked that he knew what her values were. I challenged him to let her do this exercise on her own. To his surprise, he learned new things about his wife, including that she values sustainability. This revelation impacted Alexander greatly. Sustainability was not one of his core values, but because of this exercise and discussions with his wife, he's now a champion for sustainability and supports her efforts in this field.

As a producer in the advertising world, Alexander now consciously seeks out vendors who are mindful about the environment and budgets for any extra costs. He can do this easily for smaller accounts, but big accounts were more challenging. For example, some celebrities associated with iconic brands often require such amenities as high-end travel services with high carbon footprints. He is considering ways to make them aware of their impact and shift their mindsets.

I told him a story about a chief information security officer (CISO) of a Fortune 100 company, who refused to use the company jet for one meeting when she was the only passenger and, instead, booked a flight on a national carrier. I emphasized that she could do this fifteen-minute meeting virtually and save the company even more money while decreasing the company's carbon footprint, but the CEO wanted her at the meeting in person.

I also related how other leaders, concerned about environmental impact, now take public transportation in cities such as Manhattan, London, and Paris, or use ridesharing companies, or choose fully electric vehicles aligned with the Zero Emissions incentive, one of the United Nations' Seventeen Sustainable Development Goals (SDGs). These sustainability patterns helped

Alexander realize that people are becoming conscious about caring for our planet and are taking action in their own way, if only small steps. .

Doing the personal-values exercise motivated him to implement a team-values exercise, which led to them embracing sustainability as a core value, which strengthened their meaning and purpose both at work and beyond. He is a concerned parent and wants a safe and healthy environment for his two-year-old to grow up in—that's a shift in perspective! And it grew out of his wife and him doing the personal-values exercise, which motivated him to implement a team-values exercise.

Leadership, like life, is a journey, rarely linear, often zigzagging, and always evolving. The path to self-actualization begins with clarity around your values, a willingness to learn, the courage to grow, and the gumption to lead with purpose.[3] Look to those you admire, not to imitate, but to be inspired. Let their example serve as a guide as you navigate your own authentic course, creating a better world in your own original and genuine way.

Values-driven leadership, social justice, and human rights are purposeful concepts. What are the underlying values that motivate people to advocate, elevate, and innovate for these causes? Being of service to others, positively impacting people and the planet, and, along the way, even increasing profits! The nicest part is that you can pass it on to your own circles of influence.

How do you envision a brighter future for yourself? Remember, you are a work in progress, and the goal is growth and evolution—not perfection. Take it one step at a time, and be open to figuring things out as you move forward. Embrace the journey with an open mind. Marshall Goldsmith, in his book *The Earned Life*, captures this beautifully, connecting it to Buddhist wisdom with the advice to "be open."

Now, it's your turn to explore what motivates you.

EXERCISE

Discover Your Values

Objective:
Understand your motives—what drives you.

Guidelines:
1. Identify your top three values. (If you have one more, that's fine too.)
2. Create a values statement, or a short paragraph for each value, based on meaning, purpose, and impact. You can iterate this exercise at various stages of your personal and professional life as you evolve over time.
3. Do the same exercise with your family, your team, your company, and other groups and organizations you are affiliated with locally, regionally, or globally.
4. Share your best practices with others to learn and grow together.

Summary:
Values serve as your guiding compass, helping you navigate crises with resilience and propelling personal and professional growth during times of success.

TWO

MINDFUL COMMUNICATION AND THE PRINCIPLES OF AWARENESS

Your hand opens and closes, opens and closes. If it were always a fist or always stretched open, you would be paralyzed. Your deepest presence is in every small contracting and expanding, the two as beautifully balanced and coordinated as birds' wings.

—Jelaluddin Rumi

Mindful communication is a useful concept for those who desire to communicate effectively, build better relationships, become culturally intelligent, uncover unconscious biases, develop compassion, and improve leadership skills along the way. Positive change comes from conscious awareness of yourself and others. Being mindfully present and using effective listening and speaking skills with those around you creates a harmonious communication in both personal and professional situations.

The world is becoming increasingly unified through digital technology and artificial intelligence (AI). The paradigm of top-down management continues to weaken in the era of digitalism. Innovative technologies are increasing the interconnectedness of global leadership. Tools like the Internet of Things (IoT), Generative AI, and social networks are sharing knowledge and resources to assist in resolving worldwide crises, including geopolitics, macroeconomics, and natural disasters. Many leaders across public and private sectors are learning best practices from each other and forming partnerships to eradicate big problems with big solutions, with the intention of creating a better, fairer world in alignment with the United Nations' Seventeen Sustainable Development Goals. For example, in collaboration with UN agencies, Google's *Flood Hub* uses AI and satellite data to predict floods up to seven days in advance across more than eighty countries, helping communities prepare and respond more effectively to climate-related disasters that align with SDG 11 (Sustainable Cities & Communities) and SDG 13 (Climate Action).[1] At the same time, the nature of work itself is being reorganized by hybrid environments, accelerated change, and the lasting effects of global crises, leaving many in the workforce, both new and experienced, to navigate growing uncertainty and complexity.

Now more than ever, mindful communication and expanded awareness are needed for leaders to collaborate effectively within organizations and across sectors and industries, whether in person or through virtual platforms. Once learned, you will be able to communicate more authentically based on trust to generate positive outcomes and win-win situations.

Don't you desire more meaningful, caring, and productive relationships with your colleagues, your bosses, your clients, your family and friends, and the world at large? The answer, of course, is yes. So, let's begin your journey by diving into the art of conscious communications.

In this chapter you will explore the two principles that constitute the foundation of mindful communication and the related discipline of civility, which I include because it is important that civility is not lost in the era of the IoT. Although the nature of the world is being transformed in the twenty-first century, we are all still human beings, not yet a hybrid of human-machines. The chapter is organized in four parts:

1. The first principle relates to three levels of *effective listening and speaking* (subjective, objective, and intuitive).
2. The second principle dives *into awareness of self and others* and *mindfulness*.
3. Related: Expression through *the art of civility*.
4. In conclusion: You will be asked to reflect on your inner hero's or heroine's journey as it relates to mindful communication, expanded awareness, and leadership in these times of high uncertainty.

The art of mindful communication combines effective listening and speaking with an awareness of yourself and others. Thich Nhat Hanh, a renowned Vietnamese Zen master, wrote in his book *The Art of Communicating* that once you learn to commune with yourself, you will be better able to communicate with others by using empathy and compassion.[2] This is the overarching aim of the methods described in this chapter.

For this reason, you will begin by exploring the three levels of listening and speaking: *subjective*, *objective*, and *intuitive*. Examples and practice techniques will illustrate that listening is an active process, not passive. Next, you will delve into connecting and communicating with yourself to understand mindful awareness. These two principles are the foundation for becoming a mindful communicator.

FIRST PRINCIPLE:
EFFECTIVE LISTENING AND SPEAKING

Learning how to become a mindful communicator entails moving from a subjective method of interacting with others to an objective and intuitive method.

Subjective Listening and Speaking

Most people conduct conversations listening and speaking subjectively. They focus on their own agenda and how their experiences relate back to what the other person is saying. By becoming aware of your own subjective listening and speaking habits, you can uncover unconscious biases, stemming from how you have been brought up and educated, among other things. These biases are linked to your cultural, personal, and professional values, and an awareness of them is crucial in improving how you work with others, both in person and remotely.

The following example is based on actual interactions with three young men whose communications I helped facilitate. They are computer engineers, working in product development for a healthcare AI tech company. Their job is to integrate AI software into "smart" stethoscopes that will enable users to gain more insight into cardiovascular disease—in essence, AI for the heart. One of the three men, San, is a newly promoted manager who has had to learn soft skills to become an effective team leader (a challenging task for him, as he's an "introvert and technically inclined"—his words). The first member of his team, Marc, works on-site and sits next to him; the second, Paulo, works remotely from Brazil. Paolo moved to Brazil because his wife landed a great job there, and San worries that Paolo may resign after a few months off-site.

At the office one day, San looks over at Marc's computer screen, rolls his eyes, picks up his cell phone, and texts Marc: *Hey, last week I asked you to organize your screen.* (Despite sitting right next to each other in an open-plan office layout, he hasn't even considered conducting their conversation verbally.)

Marc picks up his cell phone and texts back: *I did.*
San: *Let's figure out the best way to organize your screen after lunch.*
Marc: *Ok.*
San: *How did your convo go with Paolo?*
Marc: *No show again.*

San: *Send him a Time Zone Map.*
Marc: *Seriously, dude?*
San: *Try Slack.*

After texting furiously for several minutes, both San and Marc put down their phones and resume work without ever addressing one another verbally. As the team's external coach, I worked with them to develop better communication skills, helping them to forge a new relationship based on trust, engagement, motivation, and productivity, both on-site and virtually. To surface their communication blind spots, I had the two engineers role-play the same scenario where they had disagreed. Speaking it out loud rather than texting, they quickly noticed how much nuance was lost in written messages and how their preference for texting came from unconscious assumptions about efficiency and discomfort with direct interaction. Through this process, both San and Marc recognized that their default communication style was determined by personal preferences that were getting in the way of effective collaboration.

Furthermore, San's bias was that his way of organizing work was simply better, more structured, more logical. He didn't consider that Marc's less linear approach might suit how Marc naturally processes information. On the other hand, Marc held the unconscious belief that real-time conversations were inefficient interruptions and that messaging was more respectful of focus time, especially in a distributed, time zone–spanning team. During the role-play, both realized that their communication preferences were formed by prior work environments, cultural expectations, and unconscious assumptions about what "professionalism" looks like. That shift in awareness allowed them to cocreate new norms: when to speak live versus when to write, how to clarify expectations across time zones, and how to check assumptions before reacting. For instance, instead of assuming Paolo had simply mixed up the time zones when he missed a meeting, they began to ask more open-ended questions, recognizing that differences in communication habits and schedules might reflect legitimate preferences or constraints.

It's important to strive for awareness of your biases and false assumptions, even in the most basic conversations. As a result of the coaching process, San, as the manager and team leader, learned to be cognizant of diverse communication and working styles and agreed to work with Marc and Paolo on improving their communication skills to work together effectively going forward. In short, the best method for effective listening is to focus on the needs of the person you are listening to or speaking with, rather than on your own thoughts, responses, or preferences.

Objective Listening and Speaking

Objective listening involves focusing on what the speaker is saying without letting your opinions or feelings or agenda distort what the other person is saying. It is effective because, by perceiving and acknowledging both the speaker's statement and the feelings behind it, you let the speaker know that you have heard and absorbed what he or she has said. Practicing objective listening will increase your skill in communicating at a deeper, more meaningful level.

Let us take as an example two men working for an international company based in Bamako, Mali. Liam complains to his boss's boss, Youssouf, "Why did they hire that woman from France who's so much younger than me? She is the world's worst boss. All she does is micromanage me."

Youssef replies, "It's normal to be upset. You probably feel that you should have been promoted, rather than us hiring someone from outside as your supervisor. Thank you for letting me know about her micromanaging style. I'll have a chat with Sophia."

In this case, Youssouf demonstrated that he has listened to and understood Liam's complaint, acknowledging Liam's hurt feelings and desire to be promoted rather than focusing on the reasons for making the hire, which would be inappropriate.

An ideal scenario: Imagine that the speaker is the only person who matters to you, empathize with their emotions, and resist the urge to create interruptions by, for example, reading incoming text messages, emails, or taking calls, whether in-person or virtual.

Developing the skill of comprehending differing viewpoints will enhance your communication with people in all areas of your life, and this effective communication, in turn, will improve your relationships, which will become stronger and more positive because you created an underlying trust.

Intuitive Listening and Speaking

An intuitive listener pays attention not only to the speaker's words but also to his or her tone, manner, body language, and implicit feelings. An intuitive listener can connect what the speaker is saying to the underlying motivation for the speaker's remarks.

Sometimes the speaker will not tell the listener exactly what he or she means, and the listener must act like a detective and uncover the real message. Doing so in your professional conversations will help you to discover what is important to your interlocutors and help you differentiate between their true feelings and the professional façades they may be presenting to you and their colleagues.

Let's look at a conversation I had as an executive coach to a founder and chairperson of the board of a privately held global company, in which she was confiding to me her worries about the CEO of her company. At a board meeting, the CEO had pounded his fist on the table and declared that he wanted to "crush the competition in whatever way possible."

As the chairperson's coach, I first acknowledged the emotion behind her words by replying, "It's understandable that this bothered you." Then, analyzing the situation, I said, "It's a clash of values. You have run all your companies competitively, but with integrity. 'Crush the competition in whatever way possible' appears to imply that corruption might be involved, and that is not a method based on your value of integrity. I suggest that you have the difficult conversation with your CEO." She agreed and stated, "It's about communication, communication, communication."

In this scenario, I knew the chairman's character as a result of our long-term coaching relationship, though you do not need to know a person well to use intuitive listening skills. You must simply strive to remain mindfully present in order to understand and absorb the person's tone, manner, body language, energy, and implicit feelings. It's focusing your full attention on the current conversation without judgment or distraction, intuiting meaning beyond the words, picking up on subtle signals, and tuning in to the underlying meaning and intent of the person's message.

In this type of exchange, the speaker must have the listener's undivided attention for as long as it takes to convey the full meaning of the intended message. Practice intuitive listening and speaking with your colleagues, clients, family, and friends. Over time, you will notice that your relationships will become more caring, productive, and meaningful.

SECOND PRINCIPLE:
AWARENESS OF YOURSELF AND OTHERS

The second principle of mindful communication involves communicating with yourself and developing mindful awareness of yourself and others. It is best achieved with these five techniques:

1. Cultivate personal and professional awareness
2. Mindfulness
3. Deep breathing
4. Meditation
5. Cultivate emotional self-awareness

Self-Awareness

Self-awareness means having (1) conscious knowledge or understanding of your own character, behavior, feelings, motives, and desires, and (2) the ability to self-regulate in conversations. In my experience, when leaders begin to really understand themselves and tune in to the people around them, something shifts. This is emotional intelligence, as popularized by Daniel Goleman, in action.[3] It can often be the difference between managing and truly leading. The resulting benefits are more authentic relationships, better decision-making, and increased impact.

Emotions are never just an internal experience. They influence how you think, act, and connect with others. When feelings are aligned, the body carries more energy and vitality, the mind is grounded and confident, and the inner self is open, compassionate, and trusting.[4] These qualities naturally inspire those around you. When feelings are misaligned, the body can feel drained, the mind clouded by worry or insecurity, and the spirt withdrawn or weighed down, which can diminish your capacity to lead effectively.[5] As a leader, when you recognize these shifts in yourself and others, you can respond with greater emotional agility and create conversations and relationships that have deeper impact.

Consider a client who is a global head of a cloud-based company. Her role consists of strategic planning and leading the technical direction of a large team. Recently, her division went through a second reorganization (reorg) in a span of six months driven by economic instability and AI integrations. She had to deal with layoffs on her team, manage difficult conversations, and motivate the team toward alignment with the organization's new goals while adapting to a new normal of rapid change. As a result, she experienced high stress levels, exhaustion, and worry.

Having a great sense of humor, she joked, "I see a psy for business problems, not family! My personal life is beautiful." As she correctly put it, she was

out of balance with her body and ego/mind due to stress at work but in alignment with her soul as her wife and family brought her love and joy. Centering
herself through breathwork helped ground her, and she decided to join a friend
after work for a game of tennis. Whacking the hell out of the ball was great for
stress management. In addition, a nice three-week vacation with her family was
on the horizon to look forward to, and these things shifted her mindset back
to positivity and vitality, her normal state of being. Getting realigned with the
positive attributes of her body, mind, and soul helped her manage her emotions, effectively communicate change, and lead her team toward success. By
being self-aware, she was able to identify what feelings and behaviors to change
to scale with her team to increase impact for the organization.

It's normal to experience variations in your emotions—to enjoy positive
feelings, fall into negative feelings, and then bounce back. Exercising self-
awareness is an important tool when communicating with others. This is
especially true during unprecedented times when you experience extraordinary levels of stress. Under all circumstances, recognizing the different states
of your body, ego/mind, and soul/psyche will help you to become a mindful
leader, colleague, friend, and family member.

Mindfulness

Being mindful means staying aware of yourself and what's happening around
you while feeling steady and at ease in the midst of it. For leaders, this kind of
presence can be a game changer. It helps you respond instead of react, make
clearer decisions, and lead with greater intention.

As a leader, when you're not feeling grounded or present, your brain can slip
into survival mode. This comes from what's often called the "reptilian brain,"
the part hardwired to identify threats.[6] It tends to take over in moments when
you feel criticized, left out, disrespected, or undervalued. In those situations,
fear steps in and your amygdala, the brain's emotional alarm system, floods
your body with stress chemicals that trigger a fight, flight, or freeze reaction.

When this reflex takes control of your emotions, it hijacks your executive reasoning powers, and you lose the ability to think and communicate calmly and rationally, which of course affects how you communicate. You're no longer leading from your best self; you're reacting from instinct.

Such a state of mind will lead to poor decision-making, denial, or "paralysis by analysis" (overthinking) in leadership settings.[7] It's important to recognize when your reptilian brain takes over so you can better manage your emotions and subsequent actions. Mindfulness creates a space between stimulus and response, giving you the ability to pause before reacting. It helps you step out of that automatic fight, flight, or freeze mode, so you can regain control over your emotions and decisions. Here's an example of poor communication versus mindful communication to give clarity. In a project review meeting, the program manager says sharply, "We're 25 percent over budget. How did you let this happen?" The abrupt tone puts the project lead on the defensive, and the conversation turns tense and unproductive. A more mindful approach would be: "I noticed we've exceeded the budget by 25 percent. Can we take a few minutes to unpack what's driving that?" The second response focuses on understanding, not blame, and preserves the person's dignity while creating space for transparency, insight, and collaborative problem-solving.

By practicing mindfulness, you can quiet the noise of your primal brain and bring yourself back to a place of clarity. This shift allows you to respond thoughtfully and lead with intention, rather than being hijacked by fear or stress. In effect, mindfulness proves to be an effective strategy, calming you down, allowing you to enter the space where you can communicate rationally.

Many major organizations, such as General Mills, Aetna, Salesforce, and Google, offer mindfulness training to increase the effectiveness of their employees and the overall functionality of their workplaces. In addition to improving communication, cultivating mindfulness helps to decrease burnout and ennui, common hazards in the workplace. Its many benefits include heightened well-being, increased focus, more nuanced emotional regulation, greater empathy, and improved bodily awareness.

Meditation opens doors within yourself, helping you to dive deeper into the nuances of your own life. It can be a spiritual process and is often achieved through prayer, but it is also practiced by agnostics and atheists—meditation is for everyone. Use the meditative practice that works best for you.

Take a Moment to Center Yourself

We often underestimate how much stress and distraction we carry into conversations. Whether you're walking into a meeting or responding to a difficult email, taking just a moment to ground yourself can shift everything.

One of the simplest ways to do this is through your breath.

A former client, Steven, a fellow coach and someone living with Chronic Obstructive Pulmonary Disease (COPD), once asked me for a way to reconnect with his inner calm. I guided him through a basic breathing technique I'd learned from a yoga teacher in Manhattan: Inhale for a count of four, hold for four, exhale for four, and repeat. While breathing, I asked him to bring his attention to where he felt tension in his body and breathe into that space. He often held stress in his lower back, and as he focused on his breath, that tension began to release. He described feeling nourished, grounded, and reconnected to himself.

You don't need a yoga mat or a quiet room to center yourself. A few intentional breaths at your desk, before a call, or even during a meeting can bring you back into your body and help you respond, not react.

For others, movement can be the best path to presence: walking, dancing, running, swimming, whatever helps you feel embodied and alert. Sports and physical activity often lead people into a "flow state," a form of focused awareness that's deeply restorative.

Prayer or spiritual reflection can work the same way. For many, prayer is a kind of breathing, a moment to quiet the mind and tune in to something larger. Whether you view it as connection to God, the Divine, or simply a pause for perspective, it helps shift your mindset.

The point is not the method. It's the mindset. Choose what works for you. Then make space for reflection. Journaling can help translate inner awareness into insight. It creates a bridge between how you feel and how you show up.

In the workplace, these small, deliberate moments of centering improve your state of mind and make you a better communicator. When you're grounded, you're more able to listen, to respond thoughtfully, and to build the trust that relationships require.

Meditation

Meditation is the process of quieting the endless chatter in your mind, letting go, and listening to your own inner voice. If you begin to meditate regularly, you will eventually experience a form of peace, whatever that might mean for you. The Buddhist teachers I've met, whether from Japan, Vietnam, Myanmar, France, or the United States, say that you can meditate while sitting down, walking, or exercising. Meditating can be done for one minute, ten minutes, an hour, all day long, or even longer. It is a way to connect with your inner self, become more aware of your emotions and desires, learn to love yourself as you are, and forgive yourself. In short, it is a form of self-care.

Empathy

The last crucial element in cultivating awareness is developing an understanding of how both you and others are feeling and how we react in various situations—in effect, practicing empathy, which "is the ability to emotionally understand what other people feel, see things from their point of view, and imagine yourself in their place. Essentially, it is putting yourself in someone else's position and feeling what they are feeling."[8] We most often think of it in terms of suffering and negative events. To be noted, there are people who don't experience empathy because they have suffered from a wide variety of trauma, often early in life, which can cause them to emotionally shut down as a protective mechanism. If you are one of those people, it is important to figure out what has caused it. Once you have, you will find yourself becoming more empathetic and compassionate toward others, and this heightened awareness will in turn improve your relationships, both at work and with your family.

Let me share a personal story to illustrate how crises can shape us and deepen our empathy.

Years ago, I resigned from a job I truly loved due to a toxic workplace. I had recently gone through a difficult divorce and relocated to start fresh in a new city. Just as I was settling into my new role, I received news that someone I had once been close to had suffered a major health emergency in another country. Despite the emotional distance between us, I felt a deep, intuitive pull to be there.

I approached management and requested an unpaid leave of absence to offer support during this critical time. Initially, the request was approved. However, shortly after I arrived to help, I received a call from a supervisor demanding I return immediately. The tone of the conversation felt harsh and dismissive, and I was accused of misrepresenting my reasons for being away.

Though the circumstances were emotionally and ethically complex, I made the painful decision to return. A family member stepped in to provide care, and I will always be grateful for their strength and compassion.

When I came back to work, I was confronted and felt publicly shamed. The incident deeply unsettled me. Ultimately, others in the organization became aware of what had happened, and leadership changes were made quietly.

At the time, I considered taking legal action but ultimately decided against it. It was a deeply personal decision, influenced by my desire to move forward, preserve my career, and protect my mental health. Instead, I focused on healing. I turned to meditation, journaling, movement, and honest conversations with trusted friends. These practices helped me reflect, learn, and gradually re-center myself.

In retrospect, the experience taught me that moments of personal crisis often clarify our values and priorities. They can also plant the seeds of resilience and compassion—for ourselves and others walking through the fire.

In the end, all these techniques led to a two-fold epiphany: *Out of crises come opportunities*, and *forgiveness is all-important*. I forgave those involved. I unknowingly played a role, too, in this unfortunate dynamic. What an impactful lesson that led to my personal and professional growth!

As a result, I learned to find potential in life's disastrous moments, and my decision to embrace forgiveness allowed me to move on positively. I discovered that I had the power to pivot, adapt, and strengthen my resilience. This experience also helped me relate not only to people who had experienced "difficult bosses" or "difficult team members," but understanding suffering increased my ability to have empathy for others who have experienced crises in their lives as well as for colleagues, clients, family, and friends who are going through temporary difficulties. I understood and empathized with their suffering. Having empathy strengthened my relationships both professionally and personally.

Mindful Communication and Civility

The five practices governing the second principle—awareness of yourself and others, mindfulness, the power of deep breathing, meditation, and empathy—can assist you on your life's journey. As you use them, ask yourself how you can become a better communicator and a mindful leader. Reflect on the factors in your life that have caused you to suffer, forgive, learn, grow, and transform.

When you practice mindfulness daily, it positively influences the people around you. The strategies presented in this chapter are meant to nudge you onto the path of self-examination, which will in turn lead to better communication with others and stronger relationships based on empathy and compassion.

Of course, forging such relationships is a lifelong process. It doesn't happen all at once. Have patience with yourself and others and work to maintain steady progress. There will inevitably be bumps on the path, forks in the road, and choices to be made. But once you have connected with yourself, your ability to connect with others will increase. You will become better equipped to manage and overcome difficult situations and to create more rewarding outcomes, where everyone involved ultimately benefits.

Remember to breathe, smile, and respect each person you encounter. Keep in mind the ancient Sanskrit greeting *namaste*, which can be translated roughly as "My spirit honors the spirit within you." Honoring others with respect fosters rich communication because, in a respectful interaction, each person is mindfully aware of the other, listens carefully, and strives to understand the other's perspective. Such respect enables us to resolve conflicts, reach agreements, figure out solutions, and explore new opportunities.

Steven R. Covey, author of *The 7 Habits of Highly Effective People*, wrote, "Change—real change—comes from the inside out."[9] Self-awareness enables you to lead the life you desire and be who you want to be, and an awareness of others enables you to help them do the same, thus creating a better world for all of us. This is an outcome to strive for and cultivate over time. The future of both work and life needs mindful leaders who practice self-awareness, collaborate with empathy, and embrace civility. Leaders need to focus on the well-being of all, not just the few.

Many organizations are incorporating mindfulness, respect, and empathic communication into their routines. Civility can become a social touchstone, and this helps everyone to become more unified. Despite the strife going on in the world, you can try and build bridges to connect with others so that it becomes customary.

Being civil stems from the idea that everyone deserves to be treated with courtesy and respect. Smiling at everyone you encounter, including strangers walking down the street, is a good place to start. It's not hard to smile at people, and your smile might be just what they needed. Smiles are often passed on, which means that being positive with yourself and others will make the world around you that much more pleasant.

Civility can also help you remember the simple rules of polite, mindful conversation: *Listen with respect*; *think before you speak*; *do not interrupt the speaker*; *don't get distracted*; *ask pertinent questions*; *be genuine*; *say a kind word*; and *be grateful*. Remember that you are responsible for what you say to others—it reflects who you are. How do you want to be remembered?

A Call to Action

This chapter has been about learning to become positive and effective mindful communicators and leaders in a wide range of situations, particularly in crises. On the largest scale, embracing mindful communication is an integral part of transforming society into a unified community in which people, the economy, and the Earth itself are sustainably balanced.

On an individual level, communicating mindfully enhances your relationships with your family, friends, colleagues, clients, and social networks—even with strangers. It will help you live the life you desire, both personally and professionally. Best of all, mindful communication starts with you and then radiates outward like a beam of light, such that your actions positively influence your circles of influence.

What are you waiting for?

EXERCISE

Unveiling Your Inner Hero/Heroine: A Leadership Reflection

Objective:
To reflect deeply on your personal growth and leadership journey by exploring how mindful communication, expanded awareness, and values-based leadership have shaped your experiences, decisions, and interactions. This exercise aims to help you connect with your inner hero or heroine, uncovering insights and strengths that empower your leadership potential.

Guideline:
Journal about your inner hero's or heroine's journey as it relates to mindful communication, expanded awareness, and values-based leadership.

Summary:
Through journaling, you will examine your leadership narrative, focusing on pivotal moments of growth and challenges. By framing these experiences within the context of mindful communication, self-awareness, and values-driven choices, you'll gain clarity on how these principles influence your personal and professional evolution.

THREE

ELEVATING MINDFUL COMMUNICATION

EMOTIONS, DIPLOMACY, BOUNDARIES, AND CONFIDENCE

The single biggest problem in communication is the illusion that it has taken place.

—George Bernard Shaw

Building upon the principles of mindful communication, self-awareness, and your awareness of others requires mastering the art of managing emotions, employing diplomacy, setting healthy boundaries, and exuding confidence. Many companies have their employees take assessments, such as DISC (Dominance, Influence, Steadiness, and Compliance) and Myers-Briggs, which evaluate communication and personality types, respectively. However, you don't need to take these on your own as long as you're aware of your communication style and also whether you're introverted, ambiverted, or extroverted.

RESPOND VS. REACT:
CONTROLLING YOUR EMOTIONS

Different communication and personality types respond differently in their interactions with others. It's important to respond thoughtfully rather than react negatively. Some of my clients have had to work on controlling their reactions with their bosses, peers, direct reports, cross-functional team leaders, internal and external partners, as well as with customers. When they react, an amygdala hijack occurs in the brain, triggering useless anger, fear, and worry and preventing rational and logical thought. These reactions are often based on perceived threats rather than actual ones.

When emotions cloud judgment, they hinder your ability to stay calm under pressure and focus on solutions. The key is to take the emotions out of the equation and create dialogue based on logic, allowing everyone involved to think clearly and solve problems effectively. Reacting with strong negative emotions often causes regret that can linger for days, months, or even years, depending on whether you can forgive, apologize, and commit to better communication in the future. One way to do this is to be aware of your negative thought pattern; for example, instead of becoming overwhelmed by a project deadline and feeling anxiety, you can shift your perception, that is, reframe your mindset to the prioritization of tasks and tackle them one by one until completed. This reduces your feeling of imminent failure to one of accomplishing your goal.

To establish your ability to manage emotions, start by taking microsteps. Teach yourself to respond and not react through persistent effort over time. If you're doing your best to reframe your mindset, then you're on a path to developing trust and rapport with your entourage, both personally and professionally. It is also important to be aware of any physical symptoms you may experience related to intense emotions, such as shaking, muscles constriction in your neck, and increased blood pressure. These signs should remind you to take a time-out and breathe. Returning to mindfulness, take three deep breaths. Or excuse yourself from the conversation for a few minutes. Reengage only when you've regained your calmness.

Often, role-playing different scenarios can help prepare you to understand and not judge diverse perspectives based on other people's knowledge and experience. This practice has proven to be very effective in preparing one to respond during difficult conversations while reducing stress through an inherent shift in mindset and mood.

MANAGING EMOTIONS: A CASE STUDY

Michael, a senior executive at a software company, was advised by his boss to improve his communication style when working with a particular peer. Michael, who identified as having a challenger personality and scored high in Dominance on the DISC assessment, often found himself at odds with this colleague over how to achieve the company's ambitious goals.[1]

During our coaching sessions, Michael expressed a genuine interest in enhancing his communication skills with this internal stakeholder. It's common to encounter communication challenges with one or two individuals at work, a scenario that can also extend to family and community interactions.

Michael was confident in his authentic self, coming across as charming and philosophical in a "Tao of Pooh" manner—"focused on staying happy and calm in all circumstances."[2] He was also poetic and mindful, making the situation an intriguing puzzle. Drawing from my public relations experience, where I trained corporate executives to communicate effectively with the press, I suggested recording one of his conversations with his colleague, provided she agreed. Both parties consented.

When Michael shared the video, it was clear that tensions escalated rapidly. He appeared tense and fidgety, attempting to understand his colleague through questions, while she grew increasingly exasperated, raising her voice until she abruptly ended the conversation.

We reviewed the video frame by frame, analyzing his tone of voice, mis-understandings, and body language. Michael was unaware of his nonverbal cues until I pointed out moments like when he rolled his eyes at a particular comment. Recognizing this, he understood how these actions triggered his colleague's anger, creating a cycle of miscommunication where both parties spoke at each other defensively rather than listening to each other.

Through role-playing, we worked on improving his body language, tone of voice, and mindfulness to communicate calmly. This practice significantly improved their relationship. Michael and his colleague agreed to focus on building trust and rapport through better communication. They both adopted a more positive mindset, and Michael realized that a softer approach, rather than his usual direct and results-oriented style, was more effective with her. As we worked together, he realized that he needed to treat his colleagues in the same way he interacted with external stakeholders, i.e., with respect, dignity, contextual understanding, nonjudgment, supportiveness, and customer love. The wisdom from *The Tao of Pooh* seeped into his conscious leadership style.

Sometimes a few tweaks in one's authentic communication style can greatly enhance relationships. It all begins with awareness—the cornerstone of success.

INTERPERSONAL DIPLOMACY
AND CONFLICT RESOLUTION

Navigating the delicate art of diplomacy, whether choosing battles or striving for peace, is a skill everyone needs, personally and professionally. Conflict is inevitable, but each disagreement is unique, so each offers a chance to learn and grow.

For example, if everyone could agree to disagree about certain subjects, such as religion and politics, and move forward with problem-solving and purposeful solutions, the world would be a better place. For example, I have a dear friend who is a Republican. As I'm an independent, our political views conflict, but we've agreed to disagree, using our differences to gain a more rounded perspective that inevitably extends to various policies, macroeconomics, climate change, and geopolitics. We learn and grow from each other, achieving a more balanced outlook. Her family dinner conversations with her Democrat husband and five children don't avoid politics, but instead are lively give-and-takes and full of good humor. Contrast this with a brother and sister I know, a Republican and a Democrat, who severed their relationship over politics. They were unable to have a civil conversation on the subject, and sadly ended their relationship. This fixed mindset, marked by judgmentalism and an inability to accept different points of view, prevented them from finding common ground and maintaining their relationship. When resolving differences, it's about shifting one's mindset to embrace diversity of thought and work with it to achieve positive outcomes.

Politics is a fitting example, especially with 2024 having been a significant election year globally, involving over sixty-four countries and four billion voters. The results have shaped the world for years to come and humanity's resilience gives me hope for a more enlightened future.

Diplomacy and communication are critical in international relations, the corporate world, and interpersonal relationships. For our purposes, I'll focus on interpersonal diplomacy within organizations to navigate relationships, resolve conflicts, and foster a collaborative and positive workplace culture. This goal, though challenging, is achievable with dedication and investment from the relevant parties. For the leaders I've coached across the world, these scenarios have proven to be teachable moments, and most agree that the time and effort were worth it based on the successful outcomes that resulted. Their teams, divisions, and organizations enjoyed the benefits and advantages that came from employing empathetic diplomacy. The valuable lessons they learned enhanced their sense of belonging and inclusiveness in the workplace, which grew out of a focus on merit, excellence, empowerment, imagination, and innovation.

What are the methods? As a gentle reminder, they begin with active and empathetic listening, the mindful communication principle discussed in

Chapter Two. By attentively listening and understanding others' perspectives, you can paraphrase their messages for clarity and convey your viewpoint to find mutually acceptable solutions to the conflict or disagreement.

A client in the event industry discussed how to understand different perspectives with her team using an analogy of a bouquet of red roses. For Deirdre, the roses were red. Others saw them as pink or purple. However, one team member saw the roses as dark gray. With inquiry, Deirdre uncovered this person's color blindness. The team empathized with the color-blind member and the majority accepted the various shades perceived, with one exception. The color-blind team member objected to including red, which caused disputes until the team leader provided constructive feedback. By using the paraphrase method, Deirdre emphasized that it was understandable to see the bouquet of roses in a variety of colors due to everyone's unique interpretation of the world. There's no right or wrong. It's just an exercise to show how each person can view the same object and describe it differently. Deirdre built rapport, enhanced the team's understanding and gained their cooperation, which was essential for maintaining the team's cohesiveness, It is a great example of the benefits of interpersonal diplomacy and communication with thinking outside the box.

It's important to recognize that employing interpersonal diplomacy and mindful communication involves not only resolving conflicts and disagreements but also proactively building trust and understanding. This includes celebrating successes together, acknowledging individual contributions, and maintaining an open dialogue. Encouraging a culture where feedback is seen as a constructive tool for growth rather than negative criticism can improve relationships with all concerned stakeholders.

Patience, caring, and persistence is key. Diplomacy is not a quick fix but a continuous process of engagement, adaptation, and iteration. By committing to empathetic and active listening, fostering open communication, and valuing diverse perspectives, you will be able to navigate conflicts more effectively and build stronger, more cohesive teams. In doing so, you not only enhance your professional environments but also contribute to a more harmonious society.

The methods of active and empathetic listening, understanding diverse perspectives, and fostering a culture of constructive feedback are essential for effective interpersonal diplomacy and communication within organizations. By investing time and effort in these practices, leaders build trust, enhance cooperation, and create a positive and inclusive workplace culture. Remember, the journey of diplomacy is ongoing, requiring patience, care, and persistence, but the rewards are well worth the effort.

To stretch your growth mindset even further, let us go above and beyond with agape love. In the context of interpersonal diplomacy, it refers to an unconditional love and compassion prioritizing the well-being and understanding of others. In practice, this means treating your colleagues with respect, empathy, and genuine concern, regardless of cultural differences that may trigger miscommunications that can arise from different languages, norms, and values. By embracing agape love and the principles of interpersonal diplomacy, leaders and team members create a cooperative and positive environment, where open communication and mutual respect pave the way for effective conflict resolution and collaboration. Is my ideal of integrating agape love into employing interpersonal diplomacy an enlightened paradigm for the world over the next ten to twenty years? Or is it some crazy concept coming from outer space based on futuristic thinking? What do you think?

HEALTHY BOUNDARIES VS. OUT OF BOUNDS

Some clients are givers and people pleasers. Of course, there's nothing wrong with giving and pleasing people as long as it's not at your expense. That's why setting healthy boundaries is important for your well-being. Oftentimes, the root cause of going beyond these boundaries stems from childhood, but there are a variety of reasons for this. The following observations are based on interactions with clients who are high-functioning executives and leaders across industries, come from over seventy different countries, and practice one of the five major religions—Judaism, Christianity, Islam, Buddhism, and Hinduism—in essence, they represent a good cross section of humanity.

What makes people give to their own detriment? One client felt alienated from her parents. She was an Orthodox Jew who married a Greek Orthodox Christian in Jordan. Their children grew up embracing both religions and identify themselves as Christian-Jews. Having been rejected by her parents, she felt the need to please people—do what they wanted—in order to be liked. She said yes to everything, even if she didn't have the bandwidth to do the task or project at work. Finally, it was affecting her home life. Her loving husband repeatedly told her "it's okay to say no," to no avail.

Your loved ones know you best, but it sometimes takes a trusted coach who's unbiased for you to actually receive the message. With baby steps, she's practicing saying no and pushing back diplomatically with clear, kind communication and to her surprise, it works and people still like her. For instance, she'll thank her colleague for thinking of her but decline due to her existing workload, then recommend someone who would be a better fit. This method respectfully acknowledges the request while offering another solution. She learned that her belief, "I need to give and please people to be liked" was false. She can still give and please people when she chooses to do so as long as it doesn't drain her energy or interfere with her well-being.

It's about a balance between give and take. And it's not always the people you give to who will give back to you. Often, it comes from others as pleasant surprises. Givers and takers are everywhere. Contemplate how you work around these behavioral styles to create win-win scenarios.

Another coaching tool I use to reframe someone's mindset from over-giving and pleasing people to a healthier way of being of service is similar to servant leadership, which emphasizes the growth and well-being of others rather than yourself. Over the years, I've been delighted by many clients who embraced servant leadership as a means of managing their teams. For example, team leaders will embrace the professional development of their direct reports as well as focus on inclusivity and belonging while emphasizing well-being, thereby creating a culture of respect, empowerment, engagement, and motivation toward achieving organizational goals. I'm not dismissing other styles of leadership, but I prefer a leader who sees the big picture. Effective leaders make the best decisions for the group, not themselves. As a leader, what's your primary motivation?

Well-being. Well-being. Well-being.

Having a growth mindset, being open to constructive feedback, and becoming aware of your developmental and growth areas can help you form healthy boundaries to maintain your well-being both personally and professionally. It can be as simple as saying no when you're overworked. Thank the person for thinking of you with grace, and they'll move on to find someone else to do the task.

You may have to educate your coworkers to no longer reach out to you over the weekend because that's family time and you value quality time spent with your family as well as work-life balance. You can create messaging in your preferred means of communication, explaining that you'll get back to them Monday morning if they reach out to you on a Saturday evening. Make it clear that when it's something life-threatening or urgent—a matter that needs immediate attention or crisis management—they should of course get in touch with you on weekends. It's important to make sure your colleagues know the difference between what's a priority and what is not in order to maintain healthy boundaries.

If you're the one asking and a colleague says yes, that's great; if they say no, they, too, should provide context for you regarding their workflow or situation. If they don't do it themselves, you can politely ask what's stopping them and if they can refer someone up to the task as an alternative solution or give any other suggestion to help you out.

CONFIDENCE

Some people have it naturally, while others need to cultivate it. How? Confidence can be developed through preparedness, practice, experience, a learning and growth mindset, supportive relationships, increased competence, accomplishments, engagement in meaningful work, and living a purposeful life. These strategies not only uplift you but also inspire others. Although there are many other tools to build confidence, I focus on these due to their prevalence in my coaching practice.

One of my clients, Salma, is a senior attorney and head of industrial relations for a manufacturing company in Bangladesh. She noticed a lack of trust between the C-Suite and the factory workers. Sandwiched in between, she had to communicate effectively with both senior executives and trade union representatives. These workers demanded higher wages but felt threatened they'd be fired, even though it would violate labor laws that protected employees from unlawful dismissal.

Salma felt she had to defend the company, but she negotiated in good faith with the trade union representative to reach a fair agreement. Her communication style was mild rather than direct. She was dealing with upper management and knew she needed to speak articulately and tactfully. We worked on identifying what she needed to share with her CEO from the union representative's perspective and what she needed to share with the union representatives. We also discussed how to share her personal convictions, that the workers deserved a pay increase. This would require courage, as managing up on behalf of the unionized workforce was challenging due to leadership's perception that trade unions reduce their competitiveness. The high-wire act resulted in Salma negotiating a deal with a beneficial outcome for both parties.

We practiced role-playing to help her speak with poise and confidence, clearly communicating her heartfelt solutions. She defended her stance with facts, evidence, and the law and politely challenged authority figures when necessary. Most senior leaders value being challenged and seeing contrary points of view that lead to better solutions and positive business outcomes. She aligned agreement through mutual understanding, influence, and tactical empathy. Respecting everyone and staying true to her authentic, caring leadership style resulted in win-win outcomes that were beyond her wildest expectations. Management proved extremely understanding and there was no retaliation against workers seeking increased wages. This experience further increased her self-image as a competent, confident leader and communicator.

In Asia, I'm told, it's uncommon to lead with heart-centered leadership. However, the women I know who work there are bravely leading their teams more and more in that direction, while navigating the still dominant patriarchal paradigm.

In conclusion, the advanced principles of mindful communication—managing emotions, employing diplomacy, setting healthy boundaries, and building confidence—are essential for fostering meaningful and effective interactions. By cultivating self-awareness and empathy, individuals can navigate the complexities of personal and professional relationships with grace and authenticity. Embracing these practices not only enhances communication but also contributes to a more harmonious and productive environment. As we continue to refine these skills, we pave the way for more compassionate, understanding, and resilient communities, both within our workplaces and beyond.

EXERCISE

Mindful Communication Journal

Objective:
Enhance self-awareness, manage emotions, employ diplomacy, set healthy boundaries, and build confidence in your communications style.

Guidelines:
Reflect and write down in your journal, a notebook, or a notes app one to three significant interactions you've had personally or professionally based on the following five themes:

- **Self-Awareness:** How aware were you of your own communication style? Were you reacting or responding?
- **Emotional Management:** What emotions did you experience? How did you manage them?
- **Diplomacy:** Did you employ any diplomatic strategies? How did they affect the outcome?
- **Boundaries:** Were there any instances where you needed to set or reinforce boundaries? How did you handle it?
- **Confidence:** How confident did you feel during the interaction? What factors contributed to or detracted from your confidence?

Summary:
The purpose is to identify your communication style, emotional responses, and areas of improvement. Set goals or baby steps in those growth areas you've identified need to improve and elevate your mindful communication skills.

Best of luck with your mindful communication journaling journey!

FOUR

REINVENTING YOURSELF

TRANSFORMATION FROM WITHIN

To be yourself in a world that is constantly trying to make you something else is the greatest accomplishment.

—Ralph Waldo Emerson

Being the best version of yourself involves a process of inner metamorphosis leading to outer reinvention. There are many strategies—some will resonate, others may not, and that's okay. Practice what works for you. You'll explore the meaning and practice of self-care, resilience, and personal and professional growth in alignment with your values. Hopefully, this ignites your first step, or if you're further down the path, the thousandth step on your journey of transformation.

SELF-CARE

Can you reframe self-care as a value? Being healthy and fit? Eating nutritiously? Having a restful sleep that energizes you to start a new day? With every breath, you're experiencing "a new life," as a client of mine, who is a COO of a FinTech company based in New York, remarked. Like many of my clients, she is wise, and often I learn as much from them as they do from me. It's a beautiful exchange of experience, knowledge, wisdom, wit, and humor.

One strategy for self-care is time blocking. Set up a certain amount of time on your calendar for fitness, rest, personal time, time with family, date night, household projects, and creative endeavors. You can do the same for work, but you would focus on deep work, such as strategic planning, creating new ideas, projects, and possible solutions. Time blocking can help you create healthy boundaries. Take, for example, an ambitious young man, Bautista, an Argentinian architect, living in Valencia, Spain. In addition to climbing the corporate ladder, he's the father of two young girls, a loving husband, and responsible family man, taking care of his family as well as his wife's, and an active board member of a global nonprofit, all while studying for his PhD. All of this can be overwhelming. Recently, it led to high stress, fatigue, and illness—the body's way of making you rest to recover, avoid burnout, and allow you to refuel and move forward.

He and his wife shared family as a value, and this experience made him realize the importance of blocking out time to exercise in the morning before the children were up so he could focus on some playtime with his girls before having breakfast together as a family. The couple valued their time together, so they agreed to set up date nights and intentionally planned long-weekend excursions so they could be alone together! Since his wife was also a professional, they synced their vacation schedules—not an easy feat. It took effort, a time audit, planning, and meticulous execution, and, with effort, it worked.

Work-wise he blocked out time on his calendar for strategic planning and road mapping sustainability projects supporting energy efficient urban environments. He calculated how much time his classes, studying, writing papers, and exams would take and set aside time for that as well. He also decreased the amount of time spent on his work with the nonprofit, knowing it was a lifelong endeavor for him and he would return to it. The board agreed he could spend less time until he finished his PhD.

It pays to invest time in self-care. Remember to include the basics when under pressure, like nutrition, such as eating a plant-based diet; stress management, by engaging in some form of movement like walking in nature or by the sea; relaxation techniques through meditation; and quality sleep, turning off your cell phone. These are minor adjustments and can have a compounding effect on your well-being, stamina, and clear-headedness. The payoffs ripple out not only to you but also to your family, colleagues, and community.

RESILIENCE

A strong foundation in self-care creates the capacity for resilience, the capability of bouncing back from adversity, challenges, or setbacks. Knowing your values can be your compass to help you navigate in the direction that serves your best interests and motivates you to persevere through hardships. Your values can help you make meaningful decisions aligned with your purpose during difficult times. Living in alignment with your value system enhances your self-esteem and confidence. It's not always easy to consistently take action based on values when under pressure amidst uncertainty, but it's something to strive for to give you peace of mind.

Valentina, who works for a multinational financial services corporation, experienced uncertainty and change fatigue. When Valentina's boss's departure left a vacuum, she boldly stepped up and valiantly led her team, aligning with her values of respect, honesty, and transparency in communications. These three pillars enhanced her ability to act as the torchlight for her team. Externally she exuded calmness but internally, uncertainty made her anxious. She needed to work through her anxiety and become aware of her innate resilience.

My solution may sound simple: I suggested she write a sticky note that said, "I'm comfortable with uncertainty" and attach it to her computer monitor. She did it, and also practiced saying it until she believed it. One day, she realized she had finally become comfortable with uncertainty—a milestone. A win to be celebrated, which she did by going to a spa with her three best friends. It was a memorable experience for all. In short, Valentina learned to discern what she could control and to let go of the things she couldn't control during times of constant change. By being open to implementing new strategies, she was able to embrace being comfortable with uncertainty and achieve a newfound awareness of her innate resilience.

Reorganizations (reorgs) have become frequent occurrences. Companies downsize, leaving fewer people to do more work. Their goal is to provide shareholder value. It's quite common for someone to experience a few reorgs within as little as six months or over a span of two years. Quite often leaders leave the organization; others move to another department within the company and teams must function without leaders until a new one is found. For example, at a high-growth tech firm in the Seattle area, I witnessed a mass exodus from the C-suite down through four layers of senior management. It felt like a ship losing both its captain and key officers all at once. Those who remain must develop resiliency skills in order to avoid burnout, or stress, or, worse, depression.

Here are some other techniques to help build resilience beyond self-care: Build community with people who support you, solve problems by breaking them down into manageable steps, seek diverse perspectives for clarity of your situation, reframe challenges as opportunities for growth, practice positive self-talk, be optimistic, embrace change with agility, and find purpose by contributing to something larger than yourself, which can include volunteering for a cause you care about. Lastly, if linked to mental health challenges, seek professional help. All of these strategies can effectively help you cope with stress, adversity, and change as you build a resilient mindset.

PERSONAL AND PROFESSIONAL GROWTH

Existential crises often serve as catalysts for profound personal and professional transformations. These moments of deep reflection—when you question your life's meaning and purpose—can arise at various stages. I once coached James, a successful investment banker from London, who was navigating such a crisis. Despite reaching the top of his career, he felt unfulfilled and disillusioned with both his work and the financial system.

Through a series of self-discovery exercises, we explored his values, uncovered his dreams, focusing on what would bring deeper meaning to his life and to his family. First, with the values-based self-discovery exercise (refer to Chapter One, the Live Your Values section), he realized his family and work-life balance were most important, not the status and wealth as before. At this point in his career, James had become weary of the relentless grind—endless travel, a nonexistent work-life balance, and he felt he was missing out on precious moments with his wife and their four-year-old son. Recognizing your values helps you understand what's truly important to you and helps guide your decisions.

Second, we explored his vision for the future by identifying his passions and what brought him joy and excitement. An avid food and wine enthusiast, he recalled a long-held dream that began in his twenties: to buy a French château, restore it, and turn it into a luxury hotel with a gourmet restaurant. By identifying how he saw his life evolving and what he loved doing, he was able to envision his fulfilling and purposeful future, a recipe for success to end a midlife existential crisis.

Getting to that point required work. I encouraged James to have an open conversation with his wife, knowing such a venture would require significant changes, including relocating from London to the French countryside and to consider the effect on their son as well as his education. They reached a compromise—moving to Paris, where his wife could continue her career in fashion, and enrolling their son in The British School of Paris, which catered to children of all ages. It was the perfect balance.

Supported by his wife's enthusiasm, and with careful research, priority setting, and detailed planning, James turned his existential crisis into an opportunity for a career shift that aligned with his passion and dreams. As a family, they embraced the uncertainty of launching a new business.

Moreover, the stars aligned and investors joined the project and the luxury hotel and restaurant proved to be great successes. It was a leap of faith, but one that allowed him to live out his dream while having more quality time to spend with his family and maintain his work-life balance, his top values.

Will this venture sustain itself in the long run? Only time will tell. What's clear is that James and his family made a thoughtful, values-driven change, stepping into uncertainty with hope and optimism. Ultimately, existential crises push you to grow, embrace change, accept life's unpredictability, and help you to evolve in both personal and professional ways. Beyond existential crises, less dramatic turning points and shifts may cause you to personally and professionally grow. It may include seeking purpose aligned with awareness of your values, embracing new experiences, or joining communities of like-minded individuals. All are essential parts of the human experience.

NEURODIVERSE INDIVIDUALS

Let's begin by understanding what the term "neurodiverse" means. "Coined by Judy Singer in 1997, the concept of 'neurodiversity' acknowledges the differences in the human brain. Instead of saying people with neurodevelopmental differences—such as autism, ADHD, or dyslexia—are 'broken' or need to be 'fixed,' neurodiversity accepts that natural differences occur. People think, learn, communicate, and process things differently, and there's nothing amiss in that."[1]

I'm not an expert, but I have coached clients who are neurodivergent, most of them high functioning. Many cope with prescribed medications, talk therapy with psychologists, along with emotional and moral support from family, friends, and colleagues.

Actually, everyone can be challenged with these distractions but I wanted to express my experiences with neurodivergent individuals. The common issues I've encountered are distraction, lack of focus, hyperfocus, and the inability to track time, each of which may interfere with setting priorities.

Just as there are different types of neurodivergence, there are different manifestations. Some people fidget, twirl their hair on a Zoom call, or have some other physical or social tics. Some suffer from anxiety, depression, and insomnia. However, when an organization provides a safe space for neurodivergent employees, the workplace benefits from these individuals' heightened focus, creativity, and problem-solving skills, leading to increased productivity and innovation. This inclusive practice can increase the confidence of many neurodivergent individuals to be better versions of themselves.

Emma's experience is a powerful example of how this can play out in real life. Diagnosed with ADHD when she was an adult, Emma, a principal engineer and an excellent problem solver, explained that setting goals with action items helped her tremendously at work. It helped her to focus and be less distracted. Nevertheless, occasionally, she would veer off track and become flustered when overseeing projects. I'd nudge her to reset her goals with more realistic and achievable deadlines. She did this, and it worked to alleviate her frustration.

Deadlines can be changed; they're not always written in stone. It's best if you can shift, pivot, be agile, change course, and move on with it. She was in the process of learning this but tended to be hard on herself if she made a mistake or didn't meet her own high expectations. She was also afraid to step into her own power and have her voice heard at work with senior leadership. Emma felt loved, respected, and valued by her husband, but at work, there were a few challenges, like self-doubt and imposter syndrome, to overcome. She had a hopeful and optimistic demeanor and willingness to be coached, which was a great start.

One day, Emma was chosen by her sponsor to give a presentation to the chief technology officer (CTO). She pushed back and suggested someone on her team with better presentation skills should do it. Her mentor told her, "I want to hear your voice, have your ideas heard. You've led your team into making innovative contributions that have improved processes and systems across the company."

We worked together to get to the root cause of her reluctance to step up. Initially there were many rational excuses. Through questions, digging deeper, more excuses.

Further questioning, "What's stopping you from delivering this presentation to the CTO?"

"I never thought of myself as a leader or innovator. It's just my job."

"How can you reframe this?"

"I can be inclusive and ask my team of engineers for their input, present to the CTO, then share any insights with my team."

"You mentioned your mentor wants to hear your voice."

Silence.

A strategy teams use to uncover the root cause of something that went wrong is called the "5 Whys Problem Solving Technique," a systematic process for solving a problem by asking "why" five times or until you uncover the root cause.[2] Emma was familiar with it, so we dived in with me putting the "why" into context for each question.

"Why don't you want your voice to be heard?"

"Some colleagues might be envious."

"You remarked you'd bring back insights to your department's team and even teach, mentor, and coach them to become solutions focused to improve processes. Why would they envy you?"

"I get nervous speaking in front of people."

"Broadway performers, politicians, and lots of other speakers get nervous before speaking in front of any size of audience. It's normal and there are techniques you can use to help you get through your fear of public speaking. Returning to you not stepping into your own power—why is your inner critic or saboteur popping up?"

Pause.

I held the space for her to think but not to overthink.

"I came from a family of eight kids. I was third from the last. Not meant to be heard. I felt loved but not valued."

"That's it. How can you reframe not feeling valued in the workplace?"

Silence.

After about a minute of honoring the space between thoughts, I said, "Take a deep breath."

She closed her eyes and took a deep breath.

"Breathe in through your nose on a count of four, hold for one, then exhale through your mouth for a count of six."

She opened her eyes and came up with a strategy: "I can put a daily reminder on my phone calendar to pause and say, 'I'm valuable'—this will be one of my new goals to practice until our next session."

"How do you feel now?"

"My self-confidence went from a 1 to a 10 on a scale of 10 being the highest. I'm going to thank my sponsor for having me talk through this issue with you."

"You're wise, as appreciation and gratitude can cultivate fulfilling relationships."

That concluded our coaching session. Veering a bit off course with the 5 Whys technique but asking powerful questions, Emma got to the root cause. In the process, her increased self-confidence helped her overcome self-doubt, resulting in being energized to present with confidence to the CTO and senior leadership.

If you are neurodivergent, the following time-management tips have been tried, tested, and proven to work. You can experiment with them to determine which ones work best for you: time audits, blocking out time on calendars using color codes, writing down events by hand in a planner, creating a daily to-do list prioritizing the five most important projects (either on paper or tracked in an app), getting a trusted accountability partner at work to follow up with you in case you've missed an important task or were late to a meeting, and goal setting with follow-up actions to help keep you organized and put a structure in place.

EXERCISE

Self-Alignment Audit

Objective:
Take actionable steps toward transforming from within, leading to mean-ingful changes in your outer life in a structured yet flexible approach.

Guidelines:
1. Identify one area of your life (personal or professional) where you feel stuck or unfulfilled.
2. Reflect on your goals in this area. What does growth look like for you here? Write down one goal that excites you but also feels a bit intimidating.
3. Break out the one goal that excites you, yet a bit scary, into small, manageable steps. For example:
   - If you want to conceive a new project at work, what's the first thing you need to do (e.g., visualize how it benefits the company and its customers, research, pitch the idea, create a hackathon)?
   - If you want to focus on personal growth, what's one habit you can begin today (e.g., daily journaling, spending forty minutes quality time with your children in the morning before work, tak-ing a class)?
4. Set a timeline for each step and begin taking action, remembering to celebrate small wins along the way. There's a military saying about developing new initiatives, "Crawl, walk, run." Step-by-step moves you toward progress. Remember, progress over perfection.

Summary:
By completing this self-assessment audit, you'll not only cultivate greater self-awareness and balance, but also initiate lasting personal and professional transformation rooted in your core values.

PART TWO

THE HEART OF LEADERSHIP

FIVE

MODELING HUMAN-CENTERED VALUES

SUSTAINABILITY AND PROFITABILITY

Only by putting our humanity at the center can we truly thrive.

—Arianna Huffington

A sustainable future in leadership lies in harmonizing people, purpose, and performance guided by humancentric values. You can lead this human evolution by prioritizing the well-being of yourself, your colleagues, and your community rather than creating conditions that drive uncertainty, fear, stress, and burnout. It's a people-first mindset that is nevertheless competitive, innovative, and profitable. Leaning too far by, for example, overemphasizing profit or performance or prioritizing people without accountability will create imbalances and discontent at every level of an organization.

As leaders, you can address this holistic, humancentric approach beginning with your own spheres of influence. By role-modeling this balanced approach, you will inspire others to follow. The results are more engaged teams, healthier workplace cultures, and measurable contributions to the bottom line—all while advancing purpose-driven initiatives. Leadership rooted in human dignity and collective well-being doesn't just transform your organization; it enriches every facet of your life, from social circles to family. You are all on a quest—your hero's or heroine's journey—together with your entourage.

Success, then, is a broad concept: it's about creating the best version of you and nurturing environments in which others benefit. It's measured not just by your performance but by the positive impact you have on those around you, centered in love, empathy, compassion, kindness, and service; components of humancentric values.

I find the way many companies approach success very curious. Year after year, they reorganize by cutting up to 10 percent of their workforce, chipping away at the culture that sustains their people. This cycle of downsizing breeds uncertainty and fear, and perpetuates a pattern that seems misaligned with long-term growth. Isn't there a more effective way? To drive both revenue and innovation, a strategy that places culture at its core and fosters a learning and growth mindset? When employees feel a sense of belonging, are truly appreciated by their leaders, and see their work contributing to the betterment of humanity, they stay. They also thrive, perform at their best, and help grow the bottom line.

In my experience working with clients in the biotech and pharmaceutical industries, this truth stands out clearly. Whether it's scientists with PhDs conducting years of research into genomics exploring somatic cell editing to prevent inherited diseases, or business leaders navigating complex regulatory approvals for lifesaving drugs, purpose drives their work. Scientists strive to create breakthroughs, such as a new vaccine, while business leaders collaborate with regulatory agencies like the FDA or its global counterparts to bring anticancer drugs to market.

One client in Europe captured this sentiment perfectly when he said, "The day my company loses its purpose, I'm out." His company's C-Suite, characterized by responsible decision-making, set high aspirations balancing a people-first culture with performance and profits, and it's been working. His experience is a testament to the fact that employees desire purpose. When their core values align with the company's mission, engagement and productivity rise. Enlightened leaders at the helm recognize that people are the backbone of their organizations. Successful companies align human-centered values with purpose, profitability, and sustainable practices, ensuring not just immediate gains but long-term competitiveness.

The following case study illustrates how one global environmental non-profit successfully operationalized its values by demonstrating that when humancentric principles are deeply integrated with purpose, performance, and sustainability, they become a strategic driver of long-term impact.

"LIVING OUR VALUES," GLOBAL ENVIRONMENT NONPROFIT: A TEAM CASE STUDY

- Team Leader Challenge: How do you keep employees motivated during the third and fourth year of a five-year $130M fundraising campaign? The first and second years are about planning and building, and the fifth year homestretch is typically exciting. During years three and four, however, employees can become disengaged, resigned, or exhibit behaviors of "quiet quitting."
- Action: Cocreated an effective communications strategy and action plan with the Team Leader around "Living Our Values" in alignment with the organization's values using the values-based exercise. Team members rediscovered their core values linked to environmental responsibility and how it aligned with the organization's vision and mission. They understood their work mattered and positively impacted Earth, renewing their sense of purpose and fulfillment.
- Result: 100 percent employee engagement and motivation was achieved, because the team loved the process. They gained self-awareness and a meaningful connection to one another. Each team member gave tangible input and became motivated. They were inspired to work on team empowerment together. This challenge had been turned into an opportunity with a very positive outcome. The Team Leader's process became a best practice recognized by top management.

The team leader's achievement of meeting their fundraising goal positively impacted many conservation projects in their area of the world.

When it comes to conserving the environment through sustainable development and finding solutions to climate and biodiversity crises, organizations of all sizes are increasingly aligning their missions with environmental responsibility. A classic business school case study is Patagonia, the outdoor apparel company renowned for prioritizing social and environmental sustainability alongside profitability. Guided by the principle that people and the planet come first, Patagonia has built a reputation for ethical practices, fair labor standards, and fostering a culture that values work-life balance.

The company's commitment to sustainability is evident in its innovative use of recycled materials and initiatives like the Worn Wear program, which promotes repairing and reusing gear. Remarkably, Patagonia demonstrates that these values can coexist with financial success—it remains highly profitable while championing environmental stewardship. This demonstrates that a people-first approach, coupled with sustainability, can drive both impact and prosperity.

At a Stanford Graduate School of Business View from the Top event, former president and CEO of Patagonia, Rose Marcario, reflected on her encounter with founder Yvon Chouinard. She recalled, "Yvon had this model where he was basically saying you can have a great business, you can make quality product, but you can also do the right thing by the environment, by your employees, by your community."[1] She described it as the "most holistic vision of business" she had ever encountered.

Under Marcario's leadership, Patagonia's annual revenues quadrupled to over $1 billion, showing that prioritizing people and the planet isn't just idealistic—it's a strategy for long-term success. Patagonia stands as a beacon of how responsible leadership can align its business vision, mission, and purpose to achieve sustainability goals and engage employees and customers while maintaining financial performance.

Being a responsible business is a delicate balancing act—caring for the Earth through sustainability efforts, treating employees with dignity, serving customers with genuine care, influencing the board, engaging with activist shareholders, satisfying investors, lobbying governments, and collaborating with regulators. It's undeniably complex. But whether you're part of a small organization or a global enterprise, every positive change begins with small, intentional steps. Lead by example, reflect on what truly matters, and take action with integrity. Your efforts can spark meaningful impact.

ON HUMANE LEADERSHIP AND CONSEQUENTIAL CHANGE

The journey of responsible leadership is not only about actions but also about the impact you leave on others. Throughout history, leaders and thinkers have reminded us of the deeper values that guide meaningful change. As Maya Angelou, the renowned American memoirist and poet, so eloquently expressed: "I've learned that people will forget what you said, people will forget what you did, but people will never forget how you made them *feel*."[2]

Building on Maya Angelou's wisdom about the power of feelings, the teachings of the fourteenth Dalai Lama remind us that leading with love and compassion is not optional—it's essential for our collective survival. As the spiritual leader and Nobel Peace Prize winner eloquently states: "Love and compassion are necessities, not luxuries. Without them, humanity cannot survive." His words have proven particularly powerful, and I hope more people in the world can lean into this one: "Our prime purpose in this life is to help others. And if you can't help them, at least don't hurt them."[3] His guidance inspires us to approach leadership with care and respect, even in the most uncertain times.

The Dalai Lama's call to lead with love and compassion resonates deeply with the timeless wisdom of Mahatma Gandhi. A champion of civil rights and freedom, Gandhi believed that true fulfillment comes from aligning personal purpose with service to others. As he reflected in *Young India* in 1925: "The best way to find yourself is to lose yourself in the service of others."[4] His words reflect that a meaningful life is built on compassion, service, and a commitment to uplifting others through your unique gifts and talents.

Let's turn now from artists, spiritual and revolutionary leaders, to business leaders to show how a human-centered approach can work in organizations. Howard Schultz, former CEO of Starbucks, wrote in his book *Pour Your Heart into It: How Starbucks Built a Company One Cup at a Time*, "When you're surrounded by people who share a passionate commitment around a common purpose, anything is possible."[5] Schultz emphasized that purpose-driven work, rooted in shared values and connection, can foster innovation, engagement, and drive long-term success.

Finally, cultivating the concept that by leading yourself, you lead others and organizations, Indra Nooyi, former chairman and CEO of PepsiCo, ranked as the second most powerful woman in business by Fortune, positively impacted her company and the people who worked for it. Her authentic leadership and belief that true success comes from investing in your own self, your people, and building a purpose-aligned culture is reflected by this quote: "The distance between number one and number two is always a constant. If you want to improve the organization, you have to improve yourself and the organization gets pulled up with you. That is a big lesson. I cannot just expect the organization to improve if I don't improve myself and lift the organization, because that distance is a constant."[6] Nooyi proved that leadership is not only about bettering yourself but also elevating others and uplifting the organization by being a positive change catalyst.

I agree wholeheartedly. I too believe that helping yourself first, then others is a prerequisite for leaders. First ask, what are you doing for yourself? Then ask, what are you doing for others? But paradoxically, it is through helping others that you become more aware of how you can take better care of your well-being and learn what makes your life purposeful. Live your life with integrity while creating a positive impact on those around you.

In essence, a people-first or humanistic approach to leadership is essential for empowering people to feel valued and, therefore, motivated to achieve mission-aligned goals and sustainable success. In addition, it's important to align your purpose with a sense of well-being in what you do, echoing the balance of inner fulfillment and outward achievement.

FROM BUREAUCRACY TO HUMANOCRACY

In much of today's organizational landscape, we still see the legacy of bureaucracy, systems built on hierarchy, positional authority, and often, inequity. Since disruption and uncertainty pervade our world, these rigid structures reveal their limits. According to Gary Hamel and Michele Zanini, the authors of *Humanocracy*, a company is a humanocracy when it optimizes people's contributions to the company, rather than their obedience and production numbers. Furthermore, the most effective leaders are those who, when faced with complexity, ignite transformative change by unleashing the full potential of their people. Their call is to move beyond top-down control toward cultures grounded in trust, collaboration, contribution, and values. This approach requires leaders to prioritize human dignity and create environments where every individual is respected, heard, and valued. You can join this movement to build organizations fit for human beings while improving sustainability measures and long-term profitability.

As an executive coach with years of experience working alongside leaders in Global Fortune 500 companies and international organizations, I've had the privilege of witnessing firsthand the shift from bureaucracy to humanocracy—an evolution toward responsible business and leadership. Leaders today are redefining success by adopting holistic, people-first strategies that honor individuals' need to feel respected, valued, and heard. But how can you bridge the divide between those who hold different beliefs about how companies should be managed to foster a shared vision of humanity where everyone is seen as worthy of dignity and rights? One approach is the *whole person* model, which encourages integrating personal and professional passions into the workplace, allowing individuals to bring their full selves to the table. As complex human beings, we thrive when we embrace our diversity, promote inclusion, build equitable systems, and fulfill the innate human need to belong—a cornerstone of social connection.

The beauty of our interconnected world through the Internet of Things (IoT) brings a mosaic of cultures to learn and adapt to personally and professionally. It's opening up our minds. There are still unconscious biases relating to different groups' characteristics and work habits across 195 countries, but I've seen progress by leaders committed to understanding various perspectives and creating new models, processes, and systems so everyone can feel included and thrive.

The will is there to spark innovative ideas and turn them into actionable deliverables, creating either more inclusivity or better customer-centric products and services. Many companies have embraced the intrapreneurial culture where managers work "inside a company to develop an innovative idea or project that will enhance the company's future" because they recognize the genius of their people and let them run with their ideas to execution.[7] It may start small but if good enough, it can be rolled out regionally, nationally, then globally. Hamel and Zanini mentioned Intuit, where I've also seen it, as well as companies focused on renewable energies such as solar, wind, biomass, and hydro power worldwide. These intrapreneurs really do want to create a better world for humanity. You too can drive positive change at your company, organizations you're affiliated with, clubs you're members of, and within your family. It all begins with a single step.

Humility and Culture Change

In our complex, uncertain world, self-examination, self-awareness, and humility are essential qualities effective leaders must possess. Leaders who are humble and, at the same time, confident are often the best leaders in times of urgency and when disrupting age-old systems is required. Today, many leaders still are arrogant and bounded by their certainty and limited thinking.

Humility in leaders, on the other hand, is essential in building trust, fostering collaboration, and improving decision-making. Such leaders seek diverse perspectives and recognize that great ideas can come from anyone on the team. Humility also allows them to open a meeting by demonstrating vulnerability and by admitting a mistake, own their errors, and ask for help. Doing so signals a willingness to learn from their colleagues' expertise. It is a tactic that can also make arrogant people in the group less hostile; in essence, it opens them up to wanting to help you resolve the issue.

A willingness to admit vulnerability and ask questions, deeply listen to people, and rely on the expertise of others builds trust and breaks down resistance. When leaders shift from certainty and arrogance to curiosity and collaboration, they inspire openness and creativity in their teams. At Zendesk, they call it "humblident"—a portmanteau meaning humble yet confident.[8] The employees strive to be humblident both at the workplace and with their customers. They work hard at building positive interpersonal relationships across the company by being empathetic, and also by actively listening to their customers' concerns and feedback without forcing their own opinions—behaviors that build trust with all stakeholders. These humblident undertakings demonstrate vulnerability, curiosity, and collaboration.

Most people are naturally solutions focused. They create a psychologically safe environment by showing up as their authentic, imperfect selves—rather than trying to play the invincible superhero or heroine. Masks and façades don't serve you or those around you. Sharing your mistakes and the lessons you've learned from them, turning them into teachable moments do. Your openness inspires others to do the same, creating a culture of authenticity and openness.

One way to do this is to focus on asking "what" or "how" questions rather than "why" or "who" to promote constructive dialogue. Listen with full attention. This approach encourages clear communication, invites participation, instills confidence, sparks ideas, and builds collaboration. Over time, these behaviors will strengthen your influence and steer you toward effective leadership.

Humble leaders who prioritize human potential and empower their teams establish an environment where individuals can excel, bring their best selves to the table, and contribute meaningfully to the organization's vision, mission, and purpose, in effect balancing business responsibilities.

MOVING FORWARD

The future of work demands a new leadership paradigm—one that balances humanity, sustainability, and profitability. Technology and AI are the main components of the current transition from the Industrial Age to the Intelligence Age. Breaking down entrenched systems will face resistance, but persistence is the key. It requires adaptation, cooperation, and mindfulness across industries and societies for this revolution to ultimately elevate humankind. When you lead with integrity, champion human dignity, take action toward Earth's preservation, and prioritize well-being, you're going to catalyze meaningful change—whether it's creating greater equality, getting to net zero, or establishing a better quality of life.

The choice is yours: Complain about the status quo, or disrupt it to create a future where humancentric values, sustainability, and profitability coexist while benefiting humanity through responsible leadership and mindful-based business practices.

EXERCISE

Purpose. People. Planet.

Objective:
Embed humancentric values and Earth-centric values into your leadership practice at work, in society, and with your family.

Guidelines:
1. **Align with Values:** Lead by example, ensuring actions reflect either organizational, societal, or familial beliefs or human-centered values.
2. **Listen and Connect:** Make a conscious effort to listen to others' perspectives and concerns. Create a safe space, encourage open dialogue, and build trust through the power of humility.
3. **Lead with Empathy:** Consider the human impact of your decisions and approach challenges with compassion.
4. **Cultivate Environmental Awareness:** Encourage eco-friendly practices, implement green initiatives, and act as a responsible steward of the planet.

Summary:
In essence, this is about balancing sustainable growth with business, societal, and family success through humancentric and Earth-centric values.

SIX

LEADING WITH PURPOSE

BUILDING HIGH-PERFORMING COLLABORATIVE TEAMS

No matter how brilliant your mind or strategy, if you're playing a solo game, you'll always lose out to a team.

—Reid Hoffman, cofounder, LinkedIn

Modern management and leadership balances driving organizational success with cultivating a culture in which people thrive. High-performing teams aren't built solely on clear goals and strategies: They flourish when leaders prioritize relationships, inclusivity, and authentic connection. Whether you are an emerging leader or a more experienced one, you can enhance your skills and strategies linked to inspiring collaboration, encouraging diversity of thought, navigating conflicts with solutioning (problem solving, critical thinking) frameworks, and keeping each team member accountable and aligned with the big picture and focused on how they contribute to the organization's success. It's about becoming a positive change agent—building a better team composition, embedding complementary skill sets and expertise, creating a values-based culture, and learning to work together through frequent, open, and transparent communications based on trust to achieve strategic or even lofty goals. By leading with purpose, you can create an environment where team members feel safe and emboldened to contribute their best, leaving a lasting impact on your team and organization.

Many clients mention objectives and key results (OKRs) as a means for setting goals and clear business expectations that are aligned with the organization's vision, mission, and high-level strategy, which will then cascade down to the divisions, teams, interlinked with employees' roles and responsibilities. It's one way to balance business expectations with effective people management. There are others, but I will use this one for practical purposes. (You could also use this framework for your personal life.)

Those who already utilize OKRs can skim or skip this section, but I suggest you read the inspirational story about a former client at the end of this section, under the subhead "A Purpose-Driven Application."

OKRs

Basically, you create your action(s) to achieve your aspiration(s) based on "why" you are doing it. This creates meaning behind the execution and contribution. Stated another way, you set your **O**bjective(s) that are measured by **K**ey **R**esults focused on key initiatives and projects followed by regular check-ins and course corrections when needed.

Figure 6.1 presents a generic OKR case study in the capital goods sector.

These OKRs balance enhancing the company's own high-performance team culture with a genuine desire to help its dealership network across EMEA achieve impactful results.

As previously mentioned, OKRs frequently come up in my coaching conversations because they provide a clear framework for leaders to implement

FIGURE 6.1

Objectives Measured by Key Results via Initiatives and Projects

Objective: Cultivate a high-performing team culture within a heavy equipment manufacturer, empowering its EMEA dealership network to enhance operational execution and responsiveness to client needs.

Key Initiatives:

1. **In-house Team Development**
   - **Key Results:**
     - Achieve 90 percent team participation in quarterly cross-functional collaboration workshops by Q4 to align strategies with EMEA's market dynamics.
   - **Initiatives/Projects:**
     - Design and conduct a "Market Alignment Workshop Series" focused on EMEA's unique challenges and opportunities.

2. **Operational Efficiency for Dealership Models**
   - **Key Results:**
     - Improve dealer service efficiency metrics (e.g., response time) by 30 percent by Q4, with quarterly progress reviews.
     - Reduce operational costs by 15 percent through inventory optimization and supply chain improvements, ensuring consistent availability of critical equipment and parts by year-end.
   - **Initiatives/Projects:**
     - Establish better relationships with authentic connection to gather direct feedback on service gaps and operational improvements.
     - Refine a process optimization framework to identify and reduce bottlenecks and ensure alignment in supply chain and production efficiency.
     - Drive accountability through dashboards for real-time tracking and reporting project outcomes within dealership operations.

Courtesy of Laura Thompson.

strategies, set goals, and align their teams around what matters most while staying adaptable to shifting priorities. This tool reduces ambiguity. Its measurable nature ensures accountability and serves to track progress. Regular reviews help identify areas for improvement and adjustment. In short, OKRs keep individuals and teams agile and focused on shared, strategic goals in alignment with the organization's vision.

OKR: A Purpose-Driven Application

From a personal perspective, clients with twenty-five to thirty years of professional experience often find themselves at a crossroads, either ready to explore new ventures or prepare for the next phase of life. One client who stood out to me was planning for retirement after a successful career at the United Nations. Her objective in retirement was clear: to build a sustainable and profitable business that aligned with her values of family, community, and environmental stewardship.

To achieve this, she and her husband launched a red hot chili farm in Madagascar, integrating regenerative farming techniques in order to preserve the local ecosystem. They diversified their product lines to include chili paste, chili oil, and dried chili flakes, all packaged in eco-friendly materials to appeal to sustainability-conscious consumers.

Through their collaborative efforts with the farmers and their employees, they are establishing a family-oriented workplace culture, supporting local economies, and contributing to Madagascar's biodiversity conservation. This inspiring journey illustrates how clear objectives with key initiatives linked to measurable outcomes can drive purpose-driven transformation.

Team Dynamics

High performers don't necessarily create a high-performing team because they may not know how to collaborate and be a team player. You may recall

Reid Hoffman said, "If you're playing a solo game, you'll always lose out to a team." That may not always be true, but it frequently is. In this time of constant change, it's more important than ever to be a team player. Whether it's a reaction or response to some geopolitical, economic, or climate catastrophe, being adaptable and able to strategize, prepare, pivot, and open to possibilities at all levels of an organization is key.

Quite a few clients, from senior decision-makers to independent contributors, have gone through many iterations of reorganizations. These disruptions caused anxiety, exercised their resilience muscle, and moved some in middle management to take courses in order to gain more expertise and professionally grow in an ever-changing business environment. Some were motivated to think outside the box and create new products and services, even creating a new role for themselves, sometimes accompanied by a new title with which to roll out their pioneering initiatives. They acknowledged and moved through their fears and anxieties and agilely transitioned to the changes. They kept their egos in check and worked collaboratively with their team members and colleagues on cross-functional teams to enhance smooth transitions, often achieving more with fewer resources.

During these times of uncertainty, successful senior executives to frontline leaders learned to provide psychological safety where team members felt it was safe to express their feelings, share ideas, ask questions, and admit mistakes without fear of judgment. They established an open-door policy to address concerns and squash rumors, especially during a merger or acquisition, and focused on transparent communications to reduce misunderstandings. These leaders became more inclusive, seeking input from members with diverse perspectives before making decisions, inevitably leading to more innovative solutions.

One client in FinTech, who is open about having ADHD and being an introvert, consistently challenges groupthink with her astute questions. Senior leaders respect her questioning mind, which has led to many innovations in the company's products, thereby increasing profitability. Listening to creative individuals and those with diverse perspectives and backgrounds on your team often propels original thinking and successful results. As Sundar Pichai, CEO of Alphabet, remarked, "A diverse mix of voices leads to better discussions, decisions, and outcomes for everyone."[1]

Those leaders who practiced listening and encouraged differences of opinion succeeded; those who were arrogant, didn't listen, and told team members what to do met with resistance and did not. Healthy resolutions linked to alignment with values and cultivating collective performance leads to high goal attainment whereas focusing on a couple of star performers, playing politics, and fighting amongst teams for resources lead to low morale and reduced performance. I've observed and coached executives through these various scenarios across twenty-plus industries globally. It's a universal reaction whichever way the pendulum swings.

What is noteworthy is that those who led with values-based team leadership weathered the storms better than those who didn't because they had already established a strong foundation that kept everyone motivated, engaged, and aligned with the organization's purpose. In a way, it's leading from the inside out. The internal contextual success of these high-performing teams was based on values, trust, respect, interdependence, courage to manage conflict, and group accountability—collectively owning successes and failures. These leaders adapted to the external stimuli, adjusted to the needs of the stakeholders, provided vision, and facilitated collaboration.

Effective teams evolve and adapt in changing circumstances. Having a learning culture enhances continuous improvement and team growth. It helps when team members are held accountable for each other's professional development. One client recounted a story about attending a top military academy in the United Kingdom. The competition to be a high performer was encouraged, but the school also had an inherent policy that students had to help one another strengthen areas in which they needed develop-ment. He modestly told me that he was exceptionally gifted in physics; his mother was a renowned physicist. When a classmate needed his help to pass an exam, he mentored him to help him improve his understanding of phys-ics and pass the exam. Helping someone who needed it did not diminish my client's desire to remain competitive. As a result of this experience, he has taken this practice, paid it forward in the business world, and applied it to the teams he has led in Europe, enhancing their high team performance and effectiveness.

A good way to practice continuous learning is to have the team, at the end of a project, reflect on its recent performance by asking these questions: What went well, what went wrong, how can it be improved (e.g., processes, systems, and communications), and what actions to take going forward? These are sometimes called post-mortem meetings, retrospectives, project debriefs, lessons learned meeting, after-action review, root cause analysis, and others. These recaps help teams review, learn valuable lessons from mistakes, reiterate for upcoming projects, and celebrate wins both small and big. You can implement "retrospectives" in your personal life too. Professional and personal development can be developed in harmony.

Effective team collaboration is essential to achieving organizational goals, knowing what success looks like, and how you contribute to the larger goal. Your role and responsibilities complement your colleagues' skills and exper-tise. The best practice is to help each other rise higher by taking the time to invest in your people, whether through training, continuous education, coaching, mentoring, learning on the job, reskilling, or establishing support groups. Everyone has their own unique talents to contribute, even people con-sidered problematic—they might be in the wrong position. Your goal is to help them move into a role aligned with their strengths. Remember, it takes a team to win on the playing field. Are you going to be a participant or a specta-tor in the stands?

Choices and Challenges

People are willing to change or stretch themselves when they're aligned with a sense of purpose. Charlotte, a French native, working for a top Italian fashion house in Rome, Italy, filled in for her boss when she left for maternity leave. Her boss prepared her well to attend senior-level meetings and speak with confidence on behalf of the global marketing team. Charlotte led the digital pillar and had to delegate some of her work to her team members in order to fulfill the role and responsibilities associated with her boss's leadership position. This is a good organizational practice that allows designated and up and coming future senior leaders to learn, understand, lead, manage at a higher level, and to see how everything connects within the big picture.

Charlotte further developed her strategic thinking skills and liaised across many business units. After about three months, she said, "This might sound crazy. I want to pivot to a different role. I learned about sustainability from both the design and sourcing and the product development teams. I'd like to work in the sustainability department and strategize to make the company more environmentally conscious. Strategy and sustainability energize me. I'll be bored going back to my old role when my boss returns. I've really enjoyed stepping up in my boss's role and want to transfer this skill set to get a role in this department."

We cocreated an action plan based on her new desired direction and she rewrote her personal development plan. When her boss returned from maternity leave, she'd have this conversation with her to explore a job rotation or stretch assignment. In the meantime, Charlotte was also building a leadership pipeline for someone qualified to step into her role when she'd eventually either be promoted or move laterally into the sustainability department.

When you're bored, too comfortable, or at a crossroads in your job, it's time for you to stretch yourself and think outside the box. Ask yourself: What are your values, what are your drivers/what motivates you, what energizes you, what drains you, and what gives you purpose? You can do this in both your personal and professional life.

At work, you can ask each member of your team to do this exercise to get to know them better as human beings and to inspire them to achieve higher performance within their capabilities. Another way to manage your team is to do it together during a half-day workshop to understand where they get their energy. You're building trust and rapport through increased self-awareness and learning how everyone sees things from their perspectives. It's about valuing every person and position and motivating others to achieve their aspirations through communication, constructive feedback, encouragement, empowerment, and purpose-driven wisdom.

The Royal Navy Model: Working Enthusiastically Together Toward Shared Goals

When I was first introduced to a female three-star admiral in the United States Navy, she mentioned that Britain's Royal Navy had a model worth emulating when it came to motivation. I followed up and found out how they cultivate cheerfulness and storytelling to keep its officers motivated while covering over 140 million square miles at sea.[2] Essentially, it's the soft leadership skills that serve as the basis for high-performing collaborative teams.

I related this approach to a general manger of a fast growing team for a popular gaming platform in China. He understood that his colleagues would rather follow a cheerful leader who is approachable, confident, capable, caring, accountable, and inspirational; one utilizing soft influence to increase morale and productivity. Moods can set the pace. Who wants to work for a boss who exhibits negativity and sees only gloom and doom scenarios? Or a command-and-control style leader who makes the decisions and gives orders? He decided to create his leadership signature based on pragmatic optimism, empowering his team with autonomy, inspiring them to take emotional ownership of their roles and responsibilities while having fun. After all, he worked in a fun industry. This turned out to be his authentic leadership and management style that he had been fine-tuning through experiential learning. You're always learning and growing as you advance in your career.

Fun and cheerfulness can be implemented through banter and humor—a more relaxed way of communicating across the hierarchy while maintaining respect for one another. Another client, a commanding officer (CO), would often take a seat in the middle of an oval table during a meeting of ten to twelve officers. One junior officer remarked, "Why don't you sit at the head of the table?" The CO replied, "I'm creating an environment where everyone feels equal in his or her contributions to our strategic discussions. You know my rank." The junior officer then understood the CO's humility and ability to encourage open and constructive communications. It became a story shared informally to help build a new philosophy of democratization, inclusivity, and diversity of thought based on trust and respect. Stories can be used informally and formally in all organizations to build a culture of values.

EXERCISE

Create Your Authentic Leadership Style

Objective:
Be true to yourself to effectively lead others and organizations.

Guidelines:
1. Reflect on leaders you admire, write a few sentences or a paragraph describing your leadership and management style based on your values, strengths, and aspirations.
2. Share it with mentors and trusted peers to fine-tune it.
3. Come up with a tagline that's a memorable phrase or sentence, e.g., "Make gaming great again."
4. Walk the talk.

Summary:
When you align with purpose, you rise up and inspire others to join you. This is true of family, work, and your societal contributions.

SEVEN

BRIDGING THE GAP

STRENGTHENING CONNECTIONS WITH EMPATHY AND SELF-COMPASSION

The servant leader constantly works to help people succeed in accomplishing their goals.[1]

—Ken Blanchard, leadership expert

As an executive coach, I've witnessed firsthand how empathy and compassion transform leaders and the organizations they guide. The heart of leadership lies in serving others, not as a hierarchical mandate but as a genuine commitment to supporting those around you. Compassion creates an environment where people feel valued, understood, and empowered to thrive. When leaders embody empathy, they not only listen to the words of their team members but also strive to understand their feelings, thoughts, and perspectives, especially when they differ from their own. This willingness to step into another's shoes fosters trust, builds deeper connections, and ultimately elevates team performance. Effective leadership, at its core, is about creating a trusted space where others can flourish.

EMPATHY AND SELF-COMPASSION

In the high-stakes, fast-paced environments of Fortune 500 companies, leaders are often tasked with navigating complex interpersonal dynamics while maintaining high performance. Yet, in the pursuit of results, leaders can sometimes lose sight of their own emotional well-being and the importance of authentic connection with others. Cultivating empathy and self-compassion can transform your leadership approach, strengthen relationships, and ultimately drive sustainable success.

The Case for Empathy

Empathy is not just a nice-to-have quality; it is a critical leadership skill that fosters trust, collaboration, and innovation. Leaders who demonstrate empathy are better equipped to understand their teams' perspectives, anticipate challenges, and create environments where people feel valued and motivated to contribute, especially during times of reorganizations. Heads of departments struggle building team spirit and collaboration when there are changes across the multiple teams they lead and realize there are gaps related to improved performance and equitable contribution among their team members. Some company cultures value being nice and making people comfortable. Others value putting clients first, obligation to dissent, and consistent feedback. These are two different approaches. Leaders must be mindful of working with their company's culture and adapt.

Consider this example of a senior partner in a firm confronted with juggling demanding client projects, managing difficult colleagues, and maintaining family commitments. Despite her technical expertise and high performance, she struggled to connect meaningfully with peers whose approaches and values often clashed with her own. The disconnect created friction, leaving her feeling isolated and frustrated.

Through coaching, this executive identified empathy as a key area for growth. She began by shifting her perspective, asking, "What is the intent behind this person's actions?" This simple reframing allowed her to move beyond immediate emotional reactions, like anger and disappointment, to curiosity and understanding. It also helped her to express her emotions logically. With further probing, she became aware her own values of respect, honesty, and appreciation and realized disrespect, dishonesty, and dismissive behavior triggered her outbursts. With this new understanding, she started practicing mindfulness, being present at meetings by avoiding distractions, and exercising empathy while focusing on the middle path, a balanced approach avoiding extreme opposing perspectives to achieve collaboration with her colleagues.

We cocreated a definition of empathy linked to cultivating kindness, being curious, asking questions, and understanding different perspectives. It turned out to be a successful approach that improved her interpersonal relationships. These strategies helped her to respond thoughtfully rather than react impulsively.

The Case for Self-Compassion

High-performing leaders often extend grace and support to their teams but struggle to offer the same to themselves. Self-compassion—treating yourself with kindness, unconditional love, and acceptance during moments of perceived failure or difficulty—is important for well-being and long-term success, both personally and professionally.

One executive exemplified the challenges of self-compassion. Aiming for perfection, she set a goal to exercise daily during a hectic travel schedule in order to get into shape for an upcoming triathlon. To put things in perspective, she's doing the sprint distance that includes 1.5 kilometers of swimming, 40 kilometers of biking, and 10 kilometers of running—not an easy feat. When she couldn't meet the goal during her travels, she was hard on herself, exacerbating her stress. The coach approach, a method that emphasizes self-awareness through empowering the individual to find their own solutions, guided her to reframe her mindset and helped her recognize that temporary setbacks are part of growth and that self-compassion is a strength, not a weakness. By allowing herself to embrace imperfections, she felt re-energized.

When she implemented similar practices, she noticed a tangible shift in her interactions. Meetings became more collaborative and relationships with difficult colleagues improved. By focusing her energy on being present and empathetic, she created a ripple effect that enhanced her team's morale and performance. In addition, practicing self-compassion enabled her to resiliently navigate setbacks, inspiring her team to do the same.

Here are some tips, tools, tricks, and strategies that came out of multiple coaching sessions:

SIMPLE AND PRAGMATIC STEPS FOR CULTIVATING EMPATHY AND SELF-COMPASSION

1. **Pause and Reflect:** Before reacting to a challenging situation, take a moment to breathe, sip water, or step away. This pause creates space to process emotions and respond thoughtfully.

2. **Reframe Perspectives:** Ask yourself, "What might this person be experiencing? What are their intentions?" This mindset fosters curiosity and defuses tension.

3. **Embrace Imperfection:** Accept that setbacks are normal. Focus on progress over perfection and celebrate small wins.

4. **Invest in Relationships:** Schedule time to connect with colleagues and team members outside of high-pressure settings. Building trust in these moments can enhance collaboration during challenging times.

5. **Prioritize Self-Care:** Regular exercise, quality time with family, and moments of mindfulness can help you recharge and bring your best self to work.

Empathy and self-compassion are not innate traits reserved for a few—they are skills that can be developed with intention and practice. As a leader, investing in these qualities will not only elevate your own well-being but also empower your teams and drive meaningful results. Remember, authentic leadership starts with how you show up for yourself and others.

EMPATHY AND RELATEDNESS

Complex environments are the norm. The human-centered approach, including building the soft skills and understanding the psychological and emotional makeup of your team—what drives their communication and working styles—is important for success in demanding jobs. It begins with self-awareness: understanding yourself physically, mentally, psychologically, emotionally, and spiritually. Learning to be the architect of your own life is a lifelong journey of self-leadership. While you are in the process, progressing toward your aspirations, you're in a better place to motivate others. It's known that personal growth ignites the path to self-actualization and becoming your authentic self. Your enlightened actions serve as a torch for others to follow. Like a sleuth discovering the clues to solve a mystery, you have your unique path to uncover. Your life is a mystery until revealed step by step or sometimes by leaps and bounds. You're all fascinating individuals and you're all different, yet you are all part of the fabric of humankind and have the ability to create a better world for future generations.

Most leaders have management, financial, technical, operational, and strategic skills, yet many are deficient when it comes to self-awareness and the ability to influence from heart/brain coherence or a heart/humancentric mindset. To be effective, knowing who and what you are, being aware of your strengths and areas requiring growth and improvement is vital. The ability to change yourself before leading others to get on board with the organization's vision, mission, and strategic goals proves essential. First connecting authentically with yourself helps you be relatable and believable and not as someone faking it. Most people can see through inauthenticity, which creates distrust, which, in turn, causes discord, low morale, and low-performing teams. Your job calls for your continuous learning and growth and an open mindset so that you can create teachable moments for your colleagues through reflection, questioning, and active listening, as well as being present, humble, caring, and nurturing—in essence, the human-centered approach at the heart of leadership.

Most clients learn about themselves through assessments provided by their company. It's not perfect but it's a good start. Others complement these assessments with their spiritual inclinations and/or their family and social values. Others are self-motivated and develop and grow through self-help books, workshops, webinars, online classes, continuing education, retreats, and conferences. There's a plethora of resources to choose from for continuous learning that can be adapted to what suits you best. IoT and Generative AI (GenAI) provide additional tools with which to research, reflect, learn, and create. You can build plans to help you change your habits and behaviors with new ones to get you to where you desire to be personally and professionally.

To know yourself helps you embrace differences in others. Let's use the Keirsey Report "Temperament in the Workplace," an assessment tool that helps you discover your personality type and how it affects your performance.[2] It served as a baseline for a client's authentic model of leadership while her company was going through a reorganization. Her main temperament was Guardian with Provider as the subcategory. According to Keirsey, Guardians represent 40 to 45 percent of the population. Their natural talent is managing things smoothly in their families, businesses, and social communities through their accountable and service-oriented behavior. She also had her team take this assessment, so she could manage effectively their different temperaments: Artisan (creative), Guardian (dependable), Idealist (imaginative), and Rational (logical).

It's an art managing different temperaments. For example, Guardians may get frustrated with direct reports who are Idealists. Guardians focus on the needs of the group while Idealists like to self-develop and advocate for people to fulfill their highest potential, which could translate to being at odds with each other regarding what's best either for the individual, team, or the company. Knowing these diverse perspectives helps improve relationships, communications, and collaboration. I'm not advocating for assessments, but it can prove to be a tool to better understand yourself and others surrounding you. You may already be highly intuitive and empathetic, recognize diversity of thought, listen actively, and build solutions collectively, but based on my coaching experience, most people need to further develop self-awareness and social awareness.

LEADING FROM THE INSIDE OUT: A CASE STUDY

When Diya joined a government agency as a senior geophysicist, she inherited a team at a crossroads. In her area of expertise, climate change has caused a greater need for geoscientists to assist communities in planning risk mitigation for future flooding and storm surges with subsequent water pollution. She was brought in to help tackle these problems in new and innovative ways. Her new team had been thrown into uncertainty as a result of a recent restructuring, which the agency had hoped would boost efficiency. Fractured communication, declining morale, and an erosion of trust left team members disengaged and disconnected from their work.

Diya recognized that fixing the technical and operational challenges required a deeper shift. As someone embodying the Guardian Provider temperament, her leadership naturally stemmed from a place of care, responsibility, and alignment with core values. However, she also knew that authentic leadership starts with self-awareness. Before she could guide her team, she needed to reflect on her own purpose and principles.

Diya began by examining her own motivations and values. Why had she chosen geophysics? What kind of leader did she want to be? Reflecting on her journey, she reconnected with the sense of urgency that had drawn her to solve the challenges facing society caused by climate change. She blurted out one day, "I want to save the world." Knowing this was a grandiose aspiration, she toned it down to one of creating an environment where fellow geophysicists could work together in fun and interesting ways, while contributing to meaningful work and collaborating with multidisciplinary and community-based partners.

Grounded in this clarity, Diya made a deliberate decision: Her leadership would be rooted in connection, collaboration, and care. She believed that when people felt valued and aligned with a shared humanitarian purpose, their potential was boundless.

Building a Foundation of Trust

Diya prioritized information gathering. She held one-on-one conversations with every team member in order to understand their needs, aspirations, and concerns. She asked questions like: *What motivates you in your work? What obstacles are holding you back? What kind of team environment would allow you to do your best?* These conversations revealed what the team was happy with, what they could do better, and their eagerness to address their challenges. Team members openly shared their concerns about feeling unsafe, overlooked, and undervalued. They expressed frustration over the absence of professional growth opportunities, a lack of collaboration, and the loss of a sense of purpose or connection to a greater mission under the previous leadership team.

By deeply listening, Diya signaled that she wasn't there to impose solutions as a command-and-control leader. She was there to lead by involving them in future changes and decisions.

Aligning the Team with Purpose

Diya facilitated workshops where the team cocreated a vision for their work, seeing the big picture and how they contributed value with their expertise. Together, they defined a shared purpose: Alleviate hardships in communities due to natural disasters while delivering business value in the most efficient way aligned with the agency's mission. By grounding this purpose in their collective values of collaboration, respect, and well-being, Diya inspired the team with a renewed sense of high ownership and clear direction.

She leveraged this vision into an action plan, implemented cross-departmental meetings to encourage cooperation, and established an open data-sharing platform to improve accessibility and communication. These improvements in values-based leadership, processes, systems, and operations led to a new culture of transparency and trust that extended beyond her team to the partner teams in other departments at the agency.

Empowering through Recognition

Diya also understood that leadership wasn't about seeking the spotlight—it was about shining that light on others. She made a habit of celebrating individual and team successes, whether it was acknowledging a geophysicist data technician's evaluation at a project site or highlighting an improved process created by a junior geophysicist which made things more efficient for the team. She worked with Human Resources to establish new peer-to-peer methods of appreciation and recognition, understanding the importance of motivating her team through positive reinforcement of the values they had established as a team. Everyone's contribution mattered. Don't forget you matter as well; it's important and the inside out approach begins with self-awareness. Lead yourself first, then others, and, ultimately, the organization.

The Transformation

Significant achievements occurred. Within months, her team's culture had improved, silos broke down, entrenched fixed mindsets and resistance transmuted to learning and growth ones, collaboration increased, and clear communications flowed. The team reduced project turnaround times by approximately 20 percent through better processes. Employee engagement rose by 50 percent from a prior benchmark engagement score. More important, team members had a renewed sense of purpose, driven by the positive emotion of feeling energized. They felt more connected to their work, to their colleagues, and to the agency's mission. Diya's human-centered leadership based on values became a model for other leaders to adopt and adapt for their teams across the organization.

The Essence of Leadership

Diya's journey illustrates the power of leading from the inside out. By grounding her leadership in self-awareness, she created an environment of empathy and relatedness through inclusivity, allowing her team to align their individual talents with a shared purpose. Her story offers teachable moments for leaders:

- **Know Yourself First**: Leadership begins with self-awareness. Clarify your values, your purpose, and your authentic leadership style.
- **Listen Deeply**: Genuine connection starts with understanding the people you lead. Create safe spaces for them to share their experiences and aspirations. Be kind and candid—ask honest questions and give honest answers.
- **Align with Purpose**: Cocreate a vision that reflects shared values, ensuring that everyone feels a sense of emotional ownership.
- **Empower Through Care**: Celebrate contributions, cultivate trust, and prioritize the well-being of your team.

Diya's leadership was not only about achieving results, but also about transforming the team's culture from the ground up. By leading with heart-brain coherence—meaning being present and aware—she demonstrated her authentic style of leadership, which revolved around the humancentric approach, being values-driven, and aligning the team with purpose.

It's important to remember to find your authentic leadership style in the context of your environment and its inherent challenges and opportunities as well as your colleagues' own unique backgrounds, skill sets, needs, and complex psychological makeups. Be open. Be comfortable with unknowns. Be adaptable and willing to pivot when circumstances change. Be committed to a hopeful, sustainable humankind. Earth and society need you.

EXERCISE

A Simple Tool to Support Your Growth
in Emotional Intelligence (EQ)

Objective:
Build deeper self-awareness, self-reflection, and identify areas for growth.

Guidelines:
1. Journal daily in your Notes app or in a journal, noticing moments of strong emotion and how you reacted. Reflect on why you felt that way and how to improve your interpersonal interactions going forward.
2. Collect informal feedback from family members, colleagues, and others you trust about how your emotions and/or actions impact them. Identify patterns in their responses and how they align or don't align with your self-perception.
3. At the end of the week, review your notes and feedback, and reflect on any patterns that surprised you.
4. Repeat, review, and adjust. Assess your progress, make modifications, and celebrate small wins to stay motivated.

Summary:
This process can enhance your insight and lead to better control of your emotions, increase your people management skills, and improve your respectful communication skills.

PART THREE

RESPONSIBLE LEADERSHIP

EIGHT

ADAPTING THE MATRIX

FORWARD-PLANNING AND ORGANIZATIONAL AGILITY

While company planning typically is solidified at the end of the year, the best strategic plans are flexible by design. This enables companies to adapt to unexpected challenges or opportunities that inevitably arise throughout the year.

—Sam Reese, CEO of Vistage, December 2024[1]

Responsible leadership incorporates strategic acumen and planning. It focuses on seeing the big picture and connecting the dots. It starts with asking questions like: *Why?* or *What if?* to kick off creative brainstorming, which leads to imagining the future based on probabilities, having a vision of the future, and, even, science fiction. I recommend that you keep one foot in the present and one in the future to stay grounded, yet let yourself go wild with out-of-the-box thinking (challenging conventional thinking) as well as blue sky thinking (unimpeded brainstorming) and blue sky strategies (focusing on new and possibly cutting-edge ideas).

The blue sky methods, futures thinking, and scenario planning complement one another. Futures thinking is a qualitative approach used to create desired future outcomes by exploring possibilities; ideally that can lead to a better world. Scenario planning helps organizations quantitatively prepare for uncertainty by incorporating data to analyze future opportunities and risks and to ensure organizational agility. You can invent the future using blue sky methods, futures thinking, and scenario planning to successfully prepare for meeting uncertainty and change. All three can be part of a long-term strategic plan for navigating and preparing for the future. These practices require continuous monitoring and adaptation so that you can adjust your long-term goals, identify strategies to achieve them, and allocate resources accordingly based on new signals, trends, patterns, and insights.

Since blue sky thinking and blue sky strategies, futures thinking, and scenario planning are based on plausible alternative futures, it's necessary to be agile, experiment, iterate, and be able to navigate uncertainty as well as pivot effectively to meet situational crises. Forward-planning unleashes critical thinking and imagination on top of data-driven analytics, going a step further than *Moneyball*'s data-driven strategy. These innovative techniques help leaders build a better future for their companies across sectors worldwide. Many businesses, governments, and international organizations have already invested in forward-planning, and for those who haven't, it's time to implement flexibility, creativity, and foresight in your strategic planning, or lose your influence and competitive edge.

BLUE SKY THINKING AND
BLUE SKY STRATEGIES

Blue sky thinking is a brainstorming approach that encourages seeing the big picture and generating out-of-the-box ideas. It doesn't take into consideration constraints or risks in order to allow for futuristic innovation. For example, imagining the future of urban air mobility to address two-hour each way commutes to work where instead of sitting in your car, using an app like

Uber, you order an electric vertical takeoff and landing (eVTOL) aircraft. A driverless helicopter picks you up at home from a vertiport (landing hub) and flies you to another vertiport at work, all in a matter of minutes.

This blue sky thinking has almost been turned into reality. Today, eVTOLs, dreamt up by imaginative innovators, are being refined through actionable strategies, such as technological development, determining how they will adhere to Federal Aviation Agency (FAA) regulations and safety compliance regulations and new airspace rules, as well as infrastructure issues and marketing positioning. From vision to execution may take a decade before these companies can offer fully scale autonomous eVTOL networks in major cities.

The eVTOL industry is forward-thinking: Their vehicles are powered by renewable energy, reducing their carbon footprint. Their engineers are even working on perfecting safe AI-driven autonomous flight.

While blue sky thinking allows you to envision a world where eVTOLs revolutionize transportation, blue sky strategy provides the step-by-step execution plan to make that vision a reality. As a leader, think how you can use both blue sky brainstorming and blue sky strategies to refine the ideas into an actionable road map for building innovative products and services that will turn your vision into a competitive advantage or balance innovation with your business's goals. Start with the phrase: *Imagine a world where . . .* As you will see, there are infinite possibilities.

FUTURES THINKING

What sets futures thinking apart from blue sky thinking? Both approaches focus on exploring possibilities rather than making predictions. They share a broad perspective and encourage you to envision what could be based on foresight and imagination. However, futures thinking takes a more structured approach than blue sky. It involves collaboration within a community marked by diversity of thought, experts across sectors, imagineers, representatives across the multigenerational workforce, and people who think unconventionally. You look for signals and uncover patterns connected to the past and present to imagine new ways of doing things. Essentially, it's a long-term model to help leaders move beyond short-term goals, which can sometimes be shortsighted and limit progress in business, government, the military, international organizations, and societal institutions.

In brief, futures thinking identifies how different elements interconnect and reveal deeper forces shaping change. It empowers you to imagine and build the future while developing an actionable road map with key objectives. A ten-year horizon is often recommended, allowing you to dream big without immediate constraints. From there, you can reverse-engineer the planning process with measurable milestones. Consider the eVTOL example: These visionaries are imagining a new transportation industry while actively preparing for the future by taking strategic action today.

Signals, Patterns, Past, Present, and Future Context

At the organizational level, leaders can collectively share their observations of what's going on in their industry, the markets, geopolitics, technology, AI, quantum computing, science, and economics to uncover signals. At the Institute for the Future, they created a tool they call "signals of the future" to help develop foresight.[2] Since there is no data about the future, you have to look for signals that cause you to question what's happening, to think about what's going on behind the scenes three layers deep, or what three strategic chess moves you might take before something you believe might happen but is not yet even rumored about. Investigative journalists have questioning minds and are experts in digging deep to get the facts, the real story underlying the surface story—uncovering not only the tip of the iceberg, but also the mass below the water. Their foresight is based on the signals they observe, which they connect with historical and present patterns.

Science fiction movies, created by imaginative writers, signal what the future might look like based on patterns, current trends, and historical context. Think *Star Trek* created by Gene Roddenberry in 1966 that turned into a science fiction franchise still going today, well into the twenty-first century. The never-ending story explores different aspects of interstellar travel, intergalactic cultural interactions, and the human condition, often reflecting contemporary social issues through a futuristic lens. Roddenberry perceived a world where science, diplomacy, and cooperation sustained peace.

His signals probably stemmed from his mid-twentieth-century observation of trends, patterns, and advances that included space exploration, technological progress, cold war tensions, and the hope for peace—humanity moving beyond war, civil rights, and social change. Roddenberry cast a Black woman in a leadership role and USS Enterprise crew reflected racial and gender equality as well as interracial and intergalactic relationships foretelling an inclusive future where everyone belonged, an emerging environmental movement. The influence of great thinkers on Roddenberry is apparent throughout the series. As a writer, he utilized science fiction as a means to discuss current problems under the guise of futuristic storytelling.

Star Trek still resonates today because its themes are timeless and universal. The story evolves and adapts to modern-day challenges and remains true to its core values and themes. Since there are millions of Star Trek fans out there, the signal I'm observing is that many of you are reflecting on what it is to be human and are hopeful and optimistic that progress toward humanocracy, the betterment of humanity, and ethical stewardship of the planet is attainable.[3]

Try an action experiment with your team, your department, your organization, your family, or one of your extracurricular communities by observing signals, trends, and patterns. Consider any historical and present context, then consider how all these elements might influence the future. Be inspired investigative journalists and science fiction writers. How might these signals and patterns stimulate technological advancements in your industry, drive innovation in products or services, or open new paths for solving global challenges? Consider their potential in mediating peaceful negotiations, accelerating medical breakthroughs like cancer cures, ensuring clean water access, or enabling equitable resource distribution so that people can thrive in abundance. By training yourself and those around you to recognize and interpret signals and patterns, you can move from passive observation to active foresight, creating a better future that benefits humanity instead of merely reacting to current issues or complaining about them. Be a player, go to bat.

SCENARIO PLANNING

Each generation has its own form of uncertainty. One certainty is that the future is unknown. Because there are many unknown variables and tomorrow's conditions won't be the same as today's, you know the limits of predictions and forecasts for long-term planning. In scenario planning, you start with what might happen, envisaging multiple scenarios, both in optimistic and pessimistic ways, and leveraging diverse perspectives from the board, C-suite, line management, and experts. Royal Dutch Shell has been implementing this methodology for more than fifty years with success.[4] As a result of their success, many organizations embrace scenario planning for time spans of ten, twenty, fifty, or one hundred years depending on the industry. "Shell Scenarios ask 'what if?' questions, encouraging leaders to consider events that may only be remote possibilities and stretch their thinking."[5] It's a means of preparation to identify factors that might affect a company's future operations before making decisions and establishing action plans across their different lines of businesses. Mental agility with a focus on looking for new signals and patterns keeps your insights fresh and provides a means to update and iterate your future scenarios. The longer timeframe helps you think and brainstorm without constraints.

The following step takes into consideration data analytics, geopolitics, macroeconomics, technological advances, government regulations, social, market, and legal drivers. It's a complex process and I suggest you hire a scenario planning facilitator to guide you and your group toward effectively considering strategic options as a hedge against unknowns and uncertainty in this rapidly changing world.

Scenario planning can also help shape organizational behavior and culture. In an interview with Angela Wilkinson, a former member of Shell International's Global Scenario Team, she remarked, "Shell's corporate culture, for example, isn't like a rational machine simply marching forward: There's a culture of curiosity and learning, with tolerance for different opinions and open engagement, which comes through this process. Scenarios are developed and used by different groups in Shell for different purposes, for example, to screen investments, assess risks, manage projects, and so on."[6] Shell's core values are honesty, integrity, and respect for people and these principles align with Wilkinson's perspective related to its inherent organizational culture.

Scenario planning allied with blue sky thinking, blue sky strategies, and futures thinking are proven to be different tools for exploring multiple futures with an open mind, leveraging diversity of thought, challenging assumptions, preparing pre-decision frameworks, and helping you make resilient decisions today. These tools are valuable and may influence an organization's strategy in some areas but don't necessarily result in a business plan. That is because these models reflect possible futures and are intended to better equip you to navigate transformational change.

To help you understand further, what follows is an example of how AI could plausibly improve personal well-being and human-centered leadership in the workplace and society based on a culture of values. It's not perfect but is intended to show the rudimentary process of scenario planning—one I encourage you to try with your own team or organization as a way to stretch your mind and imagination.

AI'S ROLE IN ENHANCING PERSONAL WELL-BEING, HUMAN-CENTERED VALUES, AND LEADERSHIP

Premise

The integration of AI into workplaces and society presents significant opportunities to improve personal well-being and support a leadership style rooted in human-centered values. The extent to which AI aligns with ethical principles, organizational cultures, and humancentric practices will determine leadership models, employee engagement, and the trust barometer.[7] Given the diversity of organizations and cultures, different approaches to AI adoption will likely coexist, requiring a balance between technological innovation and the preservation of human dignity and values.

Key Uncertainties and Driving Forces

AI's role in personal well-being depends on its ability to support mental health, work-life balance, emotional intelligence, empathy, and compassion. At the outset, AI developers will need to integrate core values and ethics into AI architecture with continuous audits to ensure alignment with societal norms.[8] Benjamin Larsen, artificial intelligence and machine learning lead at the World Economic Forum, said, "AI can be a powerful tool for advancing societal well-being but only if we remain vigilant and align it with our shared values and principles."[9] Tools that offer personalized AI-driven coaching, stress management, and tailor-made learning experiences can empower individuals and improve workplace cultures. At the same time, leadership styles will be influenced by whether AI can serve as a humancentric tool or can only be used as a means to drive productivity and efficiency. AI has the potential to reduce biases and increase cultural sensitivity through education, but if misapplied, it could result in being overly data-driven at the cost of human connection.

The "what if" question is whether AI systems can reflect human ethics, moral relativism, and organizational values to help strengthen trust in leadership and institutions. Organizations that embed AI into their decision-making processes might consider whether it increases employees' sense of autonomy, purpose, and meaning in work or diminishes trust by prioritizing productivity over well-being. Regulatory frameworks could support AI's ethical role in businesses, governments, and civil society organizations. Another factor to consider is whether leaders either will integrate AI as a tool for both well-being and increased productivity or be narrow focused and use it only to drive profits.

Possible Futures

One possible future is "AI as a Copartner," where AI is deeply integrated into leadership and workplace well-being while maintaining a strong focus on human values. In this scenario, AI personalizes leadership development, incorporating tools for professionals to enhance their emotional intelligence, empathy, compassion, and relationship-building skills to develop trust and inclusive work environments. Organizations will leverage AI for personalized learning, mental health support, and values-driven decision-making, creating a more engaged and fulfilled workforce where empathy and compassion are central core principles. This is a future where AI systems and technology serve "humanity's best interests and is guided by shared values."[10]

Data supporting "AI as a Copartner" is provided by The Access Group, which surveyed over 1,100 workers across the United Kingdom across twelve sectors. The study found that 93 percent of workers acknowledged "the impact of using AI technology at work had been positive. Around 82 percent said AI has helped them produce better work, and almost 60 percent believe it has reduced their workload stress."[11] AI is helping employees in the workplace free up time from mundane tasks so that they can engage in more meaningful, high-value, purpose-driven projects, which equate with job satisfaction, work-life balance, and increased well-being. Similarly, a senior software engineering client mentioned how AI helped him with his day-to-day work so he could focus on building a high-performing team, delivering value to the organization, and maintain the team's happiness in a sustainable way.

Additional data published in the *Proceedings of the National Academy of Sciences* indicated that AI-generated messages made recipients feel more heard when it came to emotional support, evidence that AI is getting better at imitating human empathy.[12] In terms of compassionate leadership, AI tools can only assist with role-play scenarios: for example, AI can only provide insights if you input questions about an issue. Used in this way, AI augments mindful communication, builds better relationships, and can improve compassionate leadership—leading with the heart—but can't yet replace compassion because it is unable to self-reflect, experience emotions, and understand the consequences of any unethical actions. If somehow that was built into the AI system, leaders could learn how to express emotional intelligence, empathy, and compassion through AI tools to create harmony and bring out the best in everyone. It's a plausible future.

At the opposite end of the spectrum, "The Productivity Stratagem" encompasses a future where AI is widely adopted but primarily used to maximize efficiency, cost-cutting, and other transactional activities. In this scenario, AI optimizes workflows and increases productivity, leadership becomes overly data driven, leading to a decline in human connection. Employee well-being is deprioritized in favor of AI-driven high-performance metrics. As a consequence, AI's potential to enhance a culture of trust and empathy is lost. Another potential risk concerns data security and how confidential information is kept safe and secure.

A more moderate future is "Selective AI Implementation," where AI is used in targeted ways to support leadership and well-being but does not fundamentally transform workplace culture. Some leaders embrace AI-driven tools for coaching, learning, and development while others remain skeptical of its ability to help professionals improve leadership skills and well-being. While AI plays a supportive role, an established style of leadership remains largely unchanged.

Finally, "Tech Suspicion & Defiance" represents a future in which organizations and society resist AI integration due to ethical concerns and a lack of trust. Leadership remains old-style and AI's potential to enhance well-being and belonging becomes largely unexplored. This creates a divide between organizations that embrace AI with a growth mindset and those that maintain a more fixed mindset approach, leading to varied leadership experiences across industries.

Strategic Considerations

To ensure AI contributes to a culture of well-being and values-driven leadership, organizations have to approach its integration thoughtfully. Leaders may leverage AI to enhance, rather than replace, human qualities such as empathy, trust, and ethical decision-making. Businesses can develop policies that prioritize AI's role in supporting mental health, belonging, and personal growth, rather than solely focusing on efficiency. Society needs to encourage AI literacy with critical thinking skills to empower people to take ownership and positively impact human-centered leadership and well-being. What's more, in the responsible age of leadership, upskilling and training individuals to become AI literate must occur so no one is left behind. (It is noteworthy that AI has been proven to be a very helpful tool for the neurodiverse population.)

Conclusion

The future of AI's role in leadership and well-being will depend on how it is integrated into workplace culture and society across industries globally. That will require continuous ethical reflection and adaptation. It's plausible that

AI can heighten human-centered leadership by codeveloping with human beings a culture of values, empathy, belonging, and personal growth. This, too, will require intentional design and ethical implementation. Whether AI serves as a tool for values-driven leadership for the benefit of humanity or becomes a mechanism for pure efficiency will be determined by the choices made by leaders, organizations, and policymakers in the years ahead.

In summary, strategic acumen requires more than just a well-defined plan—it demands the ability to adapt, innovate, and think ahead. By integrating blue sky thinking, futures thinking, and scenario planning, leaders can cultivate a proactive mindset that embraces, rather than fears, uncertainty. These approaches encourage both creative exploration and data-driven decision-making, ensuring organizations remain agile in the face of rapid change. Forward-planning isn't about predicting the future; it is about preparing for multiple possibilities, and continuously refining strategies based on emerging trends and insights. The organizations that master this balance between vision and adaptability will not only navigate uncertainty effectively, but also shape the future to their advantage.

EXERCISE

Develop Strategic Acumen

Objective:

Continuous learning, shifting your beliefs, gaining experience, seeing the big picture, connecting the dots, and thinking unconventionally.

Guidelines:

1. Cultivate a strategic mindset by moving beyond day-to-day execution and ask, *What's going to matter most in the next three to five years? How would you think differently if you were leading at a higher level?* Consider how potential decisions might affect different parts of the business; look for the interdependencies.
2. Strengthen awareness by staying informed of industry trends, competitors' moves, customer behaviors, macroeconomics, geopolitics, and whatever else pertains to your business.
3. Develop blue sky thinking and blue sky strategies, futures thinking, and scenario planning skills to improve decision-making under uncertain conditions and making course corrections when new information emerges.
4. Enhance influence and communication skills. Share compelling stories that connect strategy to purpose, inspiring your team and key stakeholders, in sync with the organization's goals.
5. Have a growth mindset and become agile. Challenge your assumptions, explore different opinions, and ask "what if" questions. Think of strategy as a learning process, not a plan set in stone. It's okay to make mistakes. Move on.

Summary:

This framework has simplified the complexity of cultivating strategic acumen in a leadership context. Practice, experiment, make mistakes, iterate, broaden and deepen your experience, and challenge the status quo to innovate by thinking differently. As Bob Iger, CEO of Disney said, "The fusion of curiosity, creativity, and candor with an acceptance of risk and an ability to learn from mistakes—will carry you up the exponential growth curve to extraordinary business success."[13]

NINE

LEADING IN THE INTELLIGENCE AGE

A new type of thinking is essential if mankind is to survive and move toward higher levels.

—Albert Einstein[1]

Leaders must master complexity by integrating multiple disciplines in order to thrive in uncertain times, an era defined by polycrises.[2] The most effective leaders will be those who have developed the skills, mindsets, and behaviors to respond, not simply react, to simultaneous disruptions as they unfold. Such leaders are capable of strategically managing key stakeholders within their organizations through a cross-functional lens. They also are able to see the big picture, understand the interconnectivity between their business operations and global issues, such as geopolitical tensions, economic instability, and environmental catastrophes, and then integrate the various parts of the web to resolve concurrently multiple challenges.

Moreover, the Intelligence Age, marked by high-stakes challenges, demands more than technical expertise or strategic acumen; it requires a new kind of leadership, one that blends antifragility, creativity, conscious decision-making, and the ability to leverage multiple crises and thrive.[3] Today's leaders must learn to grow stronger through disruption, unlock innovative thinking in themselves, their teams, and their organizations, build an operationally resilient culture, and navigate the intersection of business, technology, politics, humanity, values, and ethics in a world that is evolving faster than ever before.

Cultivating antifragility requires deliberate actions and behaviors that embed adaptability and innovation into daily decision-making. Leaders who embody this quality actively seek challenges rather than avoid them, using setbacks as data points for learning and improvement. They foster a culture of experimentation, encouraging teams to test new ideas, do it again quickly, and embrace calculated risks. Strong antifragile leaders also develop strategic foresight, continuously scanning for emerging disruptions and positioning their organizations to capitalize on change rather than react to it. They prioritize decentralized decision-making, empowering teams to respond swiftly to challenges at all levels. Most important, they model emotional resilience and intellectual humility, that is, remaining calm under pressure, questioning assumptions, and demonstrating a willingness to pivot when circumstances demand it. By consistently applying these behaviors, leaders not only strengthen their own ability to thrive in uncertainty but also cultivate an organizational culture that transforms volatility into opportunity.

FROM PERSONAL ANTIFRAGILITY TO ORGANIZATIONAL RESILIENCE

Antifragility begins at the individual level but must extend to the organization to be truly transformative. A leader who cultivates antifragility within themselves—by embracing uncertainty, learning from setbacks, and turning disruptions into opportunities—sets the foundation for an organization that thrives under pressure. However, individual adaptability by itself is not enough. Organizations must embed antifragility into their culture, decision-making processes, and operational strategies to remain competitive in an unpredictable world.

This shift requires more than resilience; it demands a proactive approach to uncertainty in order to leverage volatility to drive innovation and strategic growth. Organizations that adopt antifragile principles move beyond disruption and turn it into their competitive advantage by translating it into real-world business strategies, from rethinking risk management to designing systems that evolve and strengthen in response to stressors.

This novel concept, introduced by Nassim Taleb in his book *Antifragile: Things That Gain from Disorder*, describes how systems, people, and organizations can grow stronger and benefit from stress, volatility, and uncertainty.[4] Later, we'll explore strategies for cultivating antifragility within your organization that build upon forward-planning and agility. This approach encourages a mindset in which challenges are turned into growth opportunities rather than risk management while maintaining stability during times of uncertainty and change.

The rapid pace of global disruption favors leaders who can influence their organizations to be adaptable and thrive in chaos, in effect better positioning themselves to lead and innovate in their respective industries. With technological advancements like AI, blockchain, and automation, it is essential that businesses embrace change. Those who can evolve and experiment with new ideas, models of thinking and strategizing, systems, and processes will emerge stronger than their competitors who stick with their traditional leadership mindsets.

Antifragility prepares leaders to be proactive in crisis management, leveraging adversity to grow and innovate, therefore going beyond the traditional model that focuses on survival or recovery. Leaders can develop personal antifragility by not only increasing their resilience—their ability to bounce back from setbacks and become mentally, emotionally, and psychologically stronger by learning and growing from the crises, mistakes, or failures that you endured and overcame—but also their ability to bounce forward to thrive and benefit from disruptions.

Antifragility is a key principle in transformational leadership. It enables you to lead through complex and high-stakes challenges in a polycrisis environment by incorporating it into the overall organizational strategy, which allows you to operate effectively and create relative balance with the aim of long-term sustainability.

LEADING WHEN UNFORESEEABLE TURBULENCE IS THE NORM

Organizations have always been challenged by unpredictable events, and they have prepared for them, often using the frameworks of futures thinking and scenario planning as part of their strategic planning to mitigate risk. These adaptive strategies work in low to moderate disruptive environments, but may not be enough when encountering heightened levels of uncertainty. The antifragile method goes beyond managing disruptions with preparedness to navigating the chaos through adaptive learning to transform the crisis into opportunity. From this perspective, antifragility challenges conventional thinking.

Consider Netflix: Not only does it disrupt markets to create opportunities for growth, but it also exemplifies antifragility by actively leveraging industry upheavals to strengthen its market position. Rather than merely adapting to change, Netflix has repeatedly anticipated and capitalized on major disruptions. Netflix's strategic evolution from a DVD rental service to a streaming giant, then to a content creator, and now into AI-driven recommendations and interactive entertainment showcases its ability to strategically transform itself by turning external threats in competitive advantages.[5] By continuously adapting its business model in response to technological advancements and changing consumer preferences, Netflix reinforces its ability to thrive in an unpredictable media industry.

In contrast, organizations that fail to adapt to shifting currents highlight what happens to fragile systems. For example, Europe's largest carmaker, Volkswagen, in 2024 announced potentially significant cost-cutting measures, including closing factories in Germany as a result of decreasing sales and lower demand for electric vehicles (EV).[6] This was a traditional response to a crisis and did not solve its problems.

Currently, Volkswagen's challenges serve as a real-time test of antifragility. The company's leadership has emphasized the urgency of adapting to changing market dynamics to avoid severe economic impacts. Although its leaders are optimistic about turning the company around, they still have to contend with competitors like the Chinese automaker who manufactures EVs, Build Your Dreams (BYD), which is planning to expand in Europe. In an economically struggling Germany, Volkswagen's birthplace, time will tell whether it can rise above the cross-currents of consumer preferences, competition, high labor costs, excessive regulation, increased tariffs, and bureaucracy. Will it adapt and emerge stronger, or will it just survive?

Antifragility would require Volkswagen to do more than cut costs; it would need to rethink its approach to innovation, supply chains, and market positioning. This could mean accelerating the development of next-generation EV technology, forging strategic partnerships, or even redefining its manufacturing and distribution models. If Volkswagen can transform these significant challenges into a competitive advantage rather than simply withstanding them, it will demonstrate antifragility. However, if it fails to evolve, sticking to legacy and traditional strategies, it risks proving the fragility of a traditional automotive giant in an era of rapid industry disruption.

Delving deeper into the weeds, Taleb believes antifragility complements robustness and resilience.[7] Amazon is a prime example, having built robust systems to withstand major disruptions. It has built a reputation for having a robust supply chain management system by leveraging advanced technology, data analytics, and an extensive logistics network to ensure fast and efficient deliveries. Its use of artificial intelligence (AI) and machine learning helps predict demand and optimize inventory placement across fulfillment centers worldwide.[8] The company's reliance on robotics and automation in warehouses enhances efficiency, while its vast transportation network, including Amazon Air, delivery drones, and third-party partnerships ensures rapid order fulfillment.[9] This seamless integration of technology and logistics enables Amazon to maintain its promise of speedy deliveries—Prime one-day and same-day shipping services—reinforcing its dominance in e-commerce.

Amazon is able to rebound effectively because of its robust supply chain management system. In addition, as Carsten Krause put it, "Perhaps one of the most significant benefits of Amazon's AI-driven supply chain is its resilience. In a world where supply chain disruptions have become increasingly common—due to factors such as geopolitical tensions, natural disasters, and pandemics—Amazon's ability to adapt quickly has proven invaluable."[10] Amazon clearly illustrates how robustness and resilience complement antifragility. Furthermore, going beyond robustness and resilience to embrace antifragility is, to use a sports metaphor, moving from a defensive stance to an offensive one, thriving amidst complexity, uncertainty, and high-impact changes. From this process, leaders become stronger and wiser.

Amazon's success demonstrates how AI, when embedded thoughtfully into operations, can create both competitive advantage and cultural benefits depicting an antifragile organization. By investing in robust, integrated data systems, Amazon ensures its decisions are informed by a complete and accurate view of the business. Automation handles routine work, boosting efficiency while allowing employees to devote more time to strategic, purpose-driven activities that align with their values. Flexibility is treated as a nonnegotiable, with AI enabling rapid adjustments to shifting market conditions.[11] Sustainability is woven into this approach, using AI to reduce environmental impact, a move that resonates with both customers and regulators. Together, these practices have not only strengthened Amazon's market position but also contributed to a workplace culture that values harmony between work and life.

The Amazon case study represents a blueprint for companies to emulate if they want to remain agile, innovative, and sustainable. It has incorporated robustness, resilience, and antifragility into its AI-driven supply chain system. Antifragility, in effect, goes beyond preparedness, agility, and resilience to a place where the leaders of an organization can transform the stressors into advantages. This proactive, innovation-driven approach ensures that organizations overcome challenges, emerge stronger, more efficient, and better positioned for future growth. It's antifragility in action.

There are organizations that survive and thrive for decades and even thousands of years! The oldest secular business in the world is Kongō Gumi, a Japanese construction company founded in AD 578, specializing in building Buddhist temples that reinvented itself over many centuries. From an innovative and antifragile perspective, it was one of the first construction companies in Japan to use concrete with wood to build temples after the Meiji Restoration in the late nineteenth century.[12] During the twentieth century, they pioneered the use of computer-aided-design (CAD) for their temple designs, demonstrating their willingness to embrace technological advances while preserving their core expertise. They are also known for their restoration of shrines, castles, and cultural heritage buildings. Kongō Gumi operated as a family-owned business for over 1,400 years until it became a subsidiary of the Takamatsu Construction Group in 2006.[13] Despite the economic pressures that led to this acquisition, it retains its identity and has continued its legacy of innovation and craftsmanship. This ability to evolve rather than resist change is a hallmark of antifragility.

Drawing a philosophical inference from Kongō Gumi's building Buddhist temples for more than a thousand years, perhaps there's an underlying, mystical correlation between Buddhism and antifragility. Buddha transformed stressors into opportunities for self-mastery and personal advancement through the creation of the Enlightened Path. His teachings were aimed at ending suffering and reaching higher states of awareness. Enlightenment (Nirvana) was gained by cultivating wisdom, ethical behavior, positive states of mind, being present in the now, and leading oneself with agility and adaptability. These practices can help you gain wisdom and clarity for your own personal and professional journey (we will further explore in the next chapter). Embrace the beginner's mind. Curiosity and thoughtful questioning are tools when diving deeper into anything, whether it's leadership, history, or the enlightened path.

CONTINUOUS LEARNING:
A PATH TO ANTIFRAGILITY

It would take two books to explain how to build flexible organizations and structures for antifragility; therefore, what follows is a targeted exploration of Peter Senge's work on organizational learning. Senge is a renowned systems thinker, organizational theorist, and senior lecturer at the MIT Sloan School of Management. In his book *The Fifth Discipline: The Art and Practice of the Learning Organization*, he outlines five core disciplines:

1. *Personal mastery*—continuous self-improvement and learning
2. *Mental models*—identifying and challenging ingrained assumptions
3. *Shared vision*—building a collective sense of purpose
4. *Team learning*—encouraging dialogue and collective problem-solving
5. *Systems thinking*—understanding interconnections within organizations[14]

Complementing antifragility are systems thinking and the ability of leaders to see the big picture, recognize patterns, and address root problems, not just the symptoms. Senge advocates for organizations to develop a culture of continuous learning, adaptability, and innovation to thrive in complex environments.

He further distinguishes between adaptive learning and generative learning in the organizational learning environment.[15] Many companies focus on adaptive learning, which teaches leaders to react to curve balls and changes. This framework assumes relative stability and uses historical knowledge and experience as a means of problem-solving and making future decisions to manage risk. It allows leaders to help their teams and organizations survive, but not necessarily thrive.

Conversely, generative thinking leans into system's thinking—understanding the interdependencies within and beyond organizations, collaborating as a collective working cross-functionally across the globe, rethinking scenarios and coming up with new ones because the underlying assumptions no longer work, and leading with agility, innovation, and evolution. Generative learning relates to Taleb's antifragility in that both are geared toward resolving high-impact events with the emphasis on innovating and redefining their organizations and industries. Netflix and Amazon are notable examples.

I coached a global head of a division of a multinational corporation (MNC), responsible for regional divisions worldwide whose company got hit by a curveball unlike anything they had ever seen—the new normal. He already was inclusive with the key stakeholders and had incorporated scenario planning, but he was still anxious and worried. During our conversation, he said, "If I can get through this and survive, I'll be fine." He hadn't heard of the antifragility method, which is a relatively new model.[16] So I summarized it and then challenged him, "What if you reframe survive to thrive?" He paused for a few moments thinking, then replied, "I love problem-solving." I pushed with him a bit further, "What about finding an innovative solution that could redefine your organization and your industry?" His creative mind lit up, I could see the light bulbs going off, as if his brain clicked with a multitude of ideas. He smiled. "I'll think about it."

A cautionary note: "While antifragility is invaluable for navigating profound changes, organizations must also ensure stability during periods of calm in order to thrive amidst dynamic shifts. Achieving this balance represents effective management on the edge of chaos."[17] It reminds me of Buddha's advice about taking the middle path, the balance between excess and asceticism. The key word is balance, a word that comes up quite often in coaching conversations. Is this a signal?

SELF-MASTERY: ENHANCING ADAPTABILITY

Besides continuous learning, upskilling, and reskilling in organizations, as a leader in the Intelligence Age, marked by the rapid advancements of interconnected technologies, leaders play an important role in cultivating mindfulness, equipping employees with tools to navigate adversity with composure, reframing challenges as opportunities for growth, and mastering complexity in the workplace. It's beneficial when mindfulness is part of an organization's educational programs as well as providing courses to develop antifragile capabilities. "It is crucial for organizations to actively nurture individual adaptability, recognizing that the collective strength of these efforts forms the foundation for the organization's ability to thrive amidst uncertainty and change."[18]

Mindfulness, adaptability, and antifragility are components of self-mastery that help you maintain balance and stability, stay clear-headed, manage your emotions to make decisions without judgment, build trust, and, as a leader, a means to inspire, motivate, and influence key stakeholders to collaborate toward achieving innovative outcomes. This new era is changing how people live and work. It is important to play your part and contribute your unique skill set, to be seen and have your voice heard, whether in the background or the foreground, depending on your innate preferences.

I encourage you to proactively choose lifelong learning personally and professionally, continuously developing your skills and capabilities, and paying it forward with knowledge sharing adding value to your team, organization, and society. Individually and collectively, investment in development metaphorically acts as a quiver of arrows, each arrow being a tool to assist you in seizing opportunities based on your values and purpose, learning and growing from adversity, becoming ever more confident with each milestone accomplished, and continuing on with your mindfulness of the necessity to thrive during these transformative times.

EXERCISE

Three Key Takeaways to Understand and Reinforce

1. *Transform disruptions into advantages (antifragility)*
2. *Shift your mindset from surviving to thriving*
3. *Recognize the need for continuous adaptive learning*

Objective:
Assess how you are building these capabilities in yourself and your organization(s).

Guidelines:
1. Identify a past disruption and analyze whether you responded with resilience or antifragility.

    Reminder: Unlike resilience, which focuses on recovery, antifragility encourages leaders to grow stronger and more innovative through adversity.
2. Reflect on a current challenge and brainstorm ways to turn stressors into opportunities.

    Reminder: Leaders who embrace antifragility don't just react to crises; they proactively leverage uncertainty to drive change.

Summary:
This exercise can help you reframe challenges through an antifragile lens. Developing antifragility requires an ongoing commitment to learning, experimentation, and recalibrating strategies in response to complexity.

TEN

CULTIVATING SELF-KNOWLEDGE

KNOW THYSELF!

Knowing yourself is the beginning of all wisdom.

—Aristotle

What does it truly mean to know yourself? Knowing yourself is the starting point to understanding yourself, others, and the world around you.

Living from the inside out, being attuned to your inner self, guided by your values, knowing your strengths, and psychological endurance allows you to manage yourself in the face of external events rather than being swept up by them. In contrast, when you live from the outside in, you risk being consumed by fear, anxiety, and doubt, which can pull you into a downward spiral, leading to the fight, flight, or freeze response. These negative emotions, however, are not inherently bad. They serve as signals, pointing toward growth, change, or the need for realignment. We all need to continuously learn, grow, develop ourselves, and determine what excites us because many of us will have sixty-plus year careers as scientific advances prolong our lives.

Every journey of self-discovery involves the ascent to peaks and the descent to valleys. The valleys represent a respite of stability and peace, where life feels relatively predictable, even comfortable. During this restful period, a sense of restlessness emerges—a sign that it's time for you to do something above and beyond what you've been engaged in at work and in life. The next step may require you to push past your limits, climb higher, and challenge long-held beliefs.

UNCERTAINTY AND OPPORTUNITY

Although our era is marked by uncertainty, it's also filled with new opportunities. Be proactive and manage your life and career. Companies try to help their employees but fall short; bosses help but are concerned with their own leadership pathways unless their values are linked to helping others. It's better to be responsible for yourself, to know your values, to create space to understand yourself, and learn to mindfully communicate and interact with others. When you act from wisdom, it sets you up for boundless success both personally and professionally.

Metaphorically, you trek up the mountain to reach the summit and stand victorious when you have achieved your bold goal. You relish the moment when you have overcome the odds and shifted your mindset to belief in yourself. Take, for example, one of my clients who set out to hike to the summit of Mount Kilimanjaro in Tanzania, the highest mountain in Africa. Doubt crept in as she compared herself to her companions. Was she fit enough? Mentally strong enough? Her inner critic whispered that she wouldn't make it. They were on their final push to the summit. The steep climb, along with the increasingly higher altitude, decreasing oxygen levels, and colder temperatures, tested her physical and mental endurance. A steady and slow ascent were critical if she was going to succeed.

The guide intuitively noticed her internal struggle and somehow knew she had the potential to keep going and not give up. He took her away from the group so she wouldn't be affected by the group dynamics as one member got altitude sickness and had to descend. He encouraged her to take one step at a time, literally one foot in front of the other, moving at her own pace. She became totally focused, present, mindful of each step, and in the zone. To her surprise, she reached the summit first, ahead of the group. As she stood at the top, she gazed at the stunning views and felt a deep sense of accomplishment as she realized that her success had little to do with comparing herself to others and everything to do with perseverance, a strong mindset, and trust in herself. Joyfully, she greeted her friends as they arrived one by one; it was an amazing moment celebrating their communal bond of friendship, love, and happiness. Since oxygen is low at the peak and conditions hard on the body, they descended to the valley and stability but with a redefined sense of themselves, one of resilience, strength, and mindfulness.

People often take treks like this to learn about themselves. Some very adventurous clients have climbed Mount Everest using South Base Camp in Nepal as their starting point. Others have hiked Northern Spain's El Camino de Santiago, a famous spiritual pilgrimage that's a thousand years old. The journey mirrors the path of self-awareness. Along the way, you encounter your strengths and weaknesses. Some qualities you refine, others you let go of because they no longer serve you.

VALUES: THE FOUNDATION OF SELF-AWARENESS

It starts with self-inquiry. Your path doesn't require a grueling trek. Find the way that suits you. Where does your journey begin? Think of yourself as the protagonist of your own story. Paint a portrait of yourself. I often ask my clients: *Who are you? How did you become the person you are today?* The answers provide a road map, tracing back to their childhood, family values, cultural influences, hobbies, and career experiences. Some environments reinforce your beliefs, while others challenge them, forcing you to define what truly matters.

Consider one client, a stockbroker, who witnessed unethical trading practices within his firm. When he questioned the reasoning behind these decisions, his colleagues dismissed his concerns, justifying their actions as standard industry practice. He couldn't ignore the conflict with his professional values. He made the difficult choice to leave, believing that integrity and a code of ethics mattered more than financial gain.

Values are the foundation of self-awareness. They evolve over time, defining your decisions, relationships, and leadership style. Each milestone, like graduating, starting a career, building a family, and engaging in professional volunteer work, offers you an opportunity for growth, revealing new layers of who you are, and refining your beingness on your journey through life. *It's not about the destination; it's about the journey.* Think of the journey as a process to be experienced and fulfilled by living in the present with mindfulness as opposed to chasing after endless goals and forgetting about what's important to you—your values, your family, your interpersonal relationships, and your wider community.

A client, a first-time father, described the experience of parenthood as *phenomenal.* At first, he was anxious, overanalyzing every possible scenario. He prepared in advance, taking parenting classes with his wife, listening to audio books and podcasts, and becoming comfortable with unknowns. Through the process, he had an Aha! moment and discovered a deeper intention of his worrying. He realized his worries weren't a weakness but a tool for thoughtful decision-making and preparedness. He shifted his negative belief about worry to one where it was useful—a positive belief. This transformation extended beyond his family; it influenced how he led his team and made choices in his professional life. Self-discovery can often be intertwined with family, work, and society. In this case, through reflection, he gained increased self-knowledge.

Many of my clients find meaning in contributing to something greater, i.e., helping others, protecting the environment, or driving innovative change within their organizations and in their industries. Values are the oxygen of knowing yourself. When you're aware of your values, your belief system, your attitudes, and your behavior, you start making conscious choices and take action based on this foundational base—your self-described pillars—that lead you toward accomplishing your tasks, goals, aspirations, and dreams with responsibility and accountability.

It's beneficial to take into account the external environment and important to factor in those elements in order to make wise decisions, but with brain-heart coherence. Leading with brain-heart harmony encompasses empathy and compassion when you must make the hard decisions. This model works in family, work, and societal situations. Also, consider that values function as your compass, guiding you through uncertainty and complexity. When you lead with self-awareness and in the ways you work best, you make choices and decisions that align with your principles, unlike when you react impulsively to external pressures.

Values in Your Workplace

Organizations, too, are influenced by values but may not necessarily walk the talk. Observe whether your company's vision, mission, and values align with your own. When your values don't align, it may cause frustration. When they align, you'll be more inclined to contribute your best and become a high performer. For example, companies that lay off employees without regard for their human impact face backlash, either from those let go or from those who remain. Talented employees question whether they're valued beyond their productivity. They question capitalism, the activist investors on boards whose short-term thinking leads them to make decisions based only on gaining share value and the leaders who cut costs by laying off a substantial part of the workforce when other methods might well be available. They question why the decision-makers aren't thinking long-term—for example, by not keeping high-performing and committed colleagues who were needed to further the team's advancement in developing an anticancer drug with fewer side effects, or those who were instrumental in keeping trusted relationships with the company's customers—but instead adopting the strategy of increasing market share at the expense of customer obsession. The scenarios are endless.

The cost of such short-term decisions is often greater than leaders anticipate. Treating people with dignity and respect isn't just ethical, it's strategic.

To see other points of view, perhaps it's true some workers are better off getting fired and finding employment at another company. An adversarial question to ask responsible leaders in the Intelligence Age might be, what could have been done to upskill or reskill those workers so that they could have stayed and found another position on another team or within another division leveraging their strengths, work styles, values, and efforts? It's known that it costs more money to hire new people and train them, but maybe the company does need fresh eyes with out-of-the-box perspectives to increase innovation and remain competitive in its industry?

There are pros and cons, but it goes back to values, treating everyone as human beings with dignity and respect, and not as bots with no feelings, family, mental well-being, health issues, or financial concerns. So, if you're going to downsize or restructure your organization, try doing it by leading from the heart with empathy and compassion, and not from the brain, rationalizing and treating these situations as transactional with no consequence to people's lives. At the collective level, we're a family of human beings interconnected through heart and mind consciousness. We're not yet in the age of transhumanism.

The Future: Values and Transhumanism

Perhaps the evolution of humanity will include transhumanism, a term coined in 1957 by Sir Julian Sorell Huxley, an English evolutionary biologist, who could also be characterized as a futures thinker. Transhumanism is a scientific philosophical movement advocating using genetic engineering, AI, and nanotechnology to improve human capabilities and transcend human limitations, like aging, disease, and physical and cognitive shortcomings. It could be a means used for human enhancement to increase strength, intelligence, and awareness.

The transhumanism movement has gained momentum since the 1980s and has become stronger in our society's zeitgeist today. Like blue sky thinking and futures thinking, transhumanism has been a common theme in science fiction where characters might be depicted as half human, half machine or having enhanced capabilities due to embedded chips in the brain or mind uploading (transferring human consciousness into digital format). Science fiction often paves the way for innovating new technologies, but technological development needs to include ethical considerations from the get-go before these new systems are put in place. This path would lead to fairness and diminish inequalities, ensuring there are no negative consequences as a result of nonalignment with society's values and making certain that transhumanism is a means to positively enhance human capabilities—a tool to benefit, not replace, humans. It's a movement that's unfolding before our very eyes. Better to be a participant, play the game, and have your voice heard so that transhumanism evolves in an ethical way, benefiting humanity.

Living from the inside out and not from the outside in is key to being able to continuously adapt to constant change and uncertainty, based on your fundamental values, which act as your compass steering you forward on your life's journey toward understanding who you are and what it means to interact with people all over the planet. You are all interdependent on your families, colleagues across and beyond your organization, and humankind in general. Perhaps, by 2050, Earth will be part of an Interstellar Alliance. How would that change your point of view about yourself in the web of interdependencies?

Knowing yourself goes beyond introspection and reflection; it's about understanding how your choices ripple out to your spheres of influence. As we move toward an increasingly interconnected future, possibly even an interstellar one, the question remains: How will we evolve while staying true to our humanity?

For futurists, the evolutionary path of humanity is not one to fear, but to embrace with hope as long as we're heart-brain coherent—that is, the heart and brain work together in harmony to advance the human condition and well-being—and intellect combines with empathy and ethical conviction to create a better world. Whether in leadership, innovation, or daily life, self-awareness is the foundation for meaningful impact. It affects how we relate to others, how we make decisions, and ultimately, how we contribute to the greater whole.

BALANCE AND SELF-KNOWLEDGE

At the core of self-knowledge is balance. Learning to navigate the highs and lows, the peaks and valleys. As Buddha advised, "Take the middle path." Striving for success is admirable, but staying at the summit indefinitely is unsustainable. True wisdom comes from knowing when to push forward and when to return to stable ground.

You can apply Buddha's wisdom to yourself, friendships, parenting, leading a team, heading a global division, a company, a board, a government, and as a citizen of the world. The aim is to find balance, decide where you belong, know thyself—the path to wisdom—and to be conscious of how your decisions affect others and the planet, lead from heart-brain coherence—intellect merged with compassion—work mindfully and effectively with others, innovate from your creative mind, and contribute what's aligned with your values for the highest good of all, benefiting humanity.

Act with integrity and remain accountable for your words and actions. It may be challenging at times, but worth the pursuit. During the process, you'll notice your self-respect and confidence have increased too. Be a responsible leader in the Intelligence Age.

EXERCISE

Getting to Know Yourself

Objective:
Understand yourself, others, and the world around you and identify
who and what has impacted you in meaningful ways.

Guidelines:
1. Write a poem or a short story, or create a short podcast, or make
    a short video (depending on your preference) as a way of getting
    to know yourself.
2. Consider your role models. They can be family members, leaders
    in your fields of interest, colleagues, or friends.
3. Incorporate your cultural background, your religious preferences,
    your country of origin, whether you've stayed in one area of the
    world or worked, lived, and traveled to many countries across
    continents.
4. Include your passions, hobbies, and what excites you.
5. End on a note of where you'd like to be in the future.
6. If you decide to write a poem, it doesn't have to rhyme.
    It can have rhythm. Whatever storytelling form you choose,
    it should have a beginning, middle, and an end. It can be realistic
    or abstract.
7. Allow yourself to be creative, have fun, and share with whomever
    you wish.

Summary:
Think of it as painting a portrait of yourself. You'll gain an understanding of yourself, others, and the world around you and how these
experiences have shaped the person you are now. Dreaming bigger,

design a future that you would like to experience, that would be in your best interest for the highest good, benefiting humanity in some unique way based on your values, attributes, and talents.

Bonus:
Voilà! An abstract portrait of myself in poetic form.

I AM

I am everywhere. I am nowhere.
I am an untethered soul,
yet responsible and accountable.
Learning and growing moment by moment,
shifting the sails aligned with the winds,
trusting my soul's journey,
traveling the peaks and valleys of life.
I am all these parts and it's OK!

—Laura Thompson

ELEVEN

BUILDING LEGACIES

LEADING WITH VALUES AND PURPOSE

*If you want to build a ship, don't drum up people to collect wood
and don't assign them tasks and work, but rather teach them to
long for the endless immensity of the sea.*

—Antoine de Saint-Exupéry

After the Great Fire of London in 1666, which destroyed much of the city, Christopher Wren, one the most renowned architects of his time, was commissioned to rebuild St. Paul's Cathedral. This parable of three bricklayers is based on a true story:

One day in 1671, Christopher Wren observed three bricklayers on a scaffold, one crouched, one half-standing, and one standing tall, working very hard and fast. To the first bricklayer, Christopher Wren asked the question, "What are you doing?" to which the bricklayer replied, "I'm a bricklayer. I'm working hard laying bricks to feed my family." The second bricklayer, responded, "I'm a builder. I'm building a wall." But the third bricklayer, the most productive of the three and the future leader of the group, when asked the question, "What are you doing?" replied with a gleam in his eye, "I'm a cathedral builder. I'm building a great cathedral to The Almighty."[1]

A version of this parable or "vision" story, told across cultures and generations, illustrates a profound truth: How we perceive our work shapes our motivation, our impact, and our legacy. The first bricklayer saw his job as a necessity, the second as a profession, but the third—he saw a purpose and found his calling.

Leaders tell this story to inspire teams to think beyond daily tasks and align their efforts with a greater vision. It challenges individuals to move beyond tactical execution and see their contributions as part of something larger—an organization's mission, values, and long-term aspirations. Stories like this resonate because they connect logic with emotion, strategy with purpose. They unlock creativity, guiding teams toward bold ideas in brainstorming sessions, futures thinking, scenario planning, and antifragility practices.

The idea of building something that stands the test of time unites people around a common goal. It transforms work from obligation into meaning. When people see themselves as cathedral builders rather than bricklayers, they take emotional ownership of their contributions. They innovate. They push boundaries. They bring personal mastery to their craft. An added benefit is that when leaders cultivate this mindset, they don't need to micromanage. They naturally empower others on the road to success.

This lesson transcends time and industry. Consider Kongō Gumi, the Japanese construction company that built Buddhist temples for over 1,400 years. Its enduring legacy went beyond carpentry and construction to one of vision, craftsmanship, and a commitment to something greater, generation after generation.

At its core, this parable highlights how values and purpose shape your work and, ultimately, your lives. Most people seek to make a positive impact, one that extends beyond themselves. Again and again, my clients have shared a common sentiment: "It makes me feel good to help others." That feeling is a byproduct of success based on values and purpose. Helping others grow, discovering their values, and finding purpose can be a joyful calling. The challenge for leaders and for each of you is to guide others toward their own "cathedral."

As Martin Luther King Jr. wrote: "If a man is called to be a street sweeper, he should sweep streets even as Michelangelo painted, or Beethoven composed music, or Shakespeare wrote poetry. He should sweep streets so well that all the hosts of heaven and earth will pause to say, here lived a great street sweeper who did his job well."[2]

How you see your work is a choice. You can focus on short-term tasks, or you can embrace the broader vision that gives life meaning. The responsible leader helps others discover their purpose. Responsible individuals ask themselves: *What monument am I building?*

Now, *what's stopping you?*

EXERCISE

Defining Your Cathedral or Monument

Objective:

To help you and your team connect daily work to a greater purpose, fostering motivation, ownership, and long-term impact.

Guidelines:

1. **Reflect:** Think about your current role or a significant project. Ask yourself:
   - Am I laying bricks, building a wall, or constructing a cathedral or a monument?
   - What is the larger impact of my work beyond my immediate tasks?
2. **Define Your Vision:** Write a brief statement describing your "cathedral" or "monument" to understand and realize the enduring impact of your work. Consider:
   - Who benefits from what you do?
   - What legacy do you hope to leave?
   - How does your work align with your values and purpose?
3. **Shift Perspective:** Imagine you are explaining your work to a new team member. Instead of describing your tasks, frame it in terms of the bigger picture. For example:
   - Instead of "I lead projects," try "I help create solutions that make gaming development great again."
4. **Take Action:** Identify one change you can make this week to reinforce your purpose, whether it's mentoring a colleague, refining a process, or sharing your vision with your team.

Summary:

What cathedral or monument are you building? I encourage you to reframe your work and life by connecting daily tasks to a larger purpose. By defining your "cathedral" or "monument" and aligning your efforts with long-term impact, you can create a culture rooted in values, motivation, personal ownership, and meaning. It challenges you to lead with purpose and inspire others to do the same, whether it is your family, your colleagues, or your community.

PART FOUR

REFLECTIONS ON COACHING

TWELVE

EIGHTEEN SHORT TAKES ON UNIVERSAL THEMES

A mind that is stretched by a new experience can never go back to its old dimensions.

—Oliver Wendell Holmes Jr.

THE INNER WORK OF TRANSFORMATIONAL LEADERSHIP

Leadership that transforms people and organizational cultures doesn't start in the boardroom. It begins in the inner landscapes of your thoughts, emotions, beliefs, and values. These universal themes explore that inner terrain, where personal growth meets professional impact. Each short take offers a fresh lens on a different dimension of leadership from the inside out, whether it's harnessing the strengths of empathy, recalibrating intuition, letting go of guilt, or reimagining what success looks like. They're not abstract theories. They're invitations to experiment with your own mindset, question inherited assumptions, and practice new ways of being that ripple outward to others.

You'll see how qualities often overlooked in traditional leadership articles and books, such as sensitivity, self-compassion, emotional intelligence, and authenticity can become your most powerful tools when anchored in clear values. You'll also confront the challenges that come with them, from navigating conflict to influencing without formal authority to rewriting the unspoken rules of the game.

Taken together, these pieces form a road map for the inner work that creates outer change. They'll remind you that transformational leadership is less about having all the answers and more about cultivating the courage, self-awareness, and adaptability to keep learning about yourselves, about others, and about the organizations you lead.

TAKE 1: THE EMPATH'S EDGE:
ITS STRENGTHS AND STRUGGLES

Most people are navigating complex relationships within their organizations, their families, and society at large. A valuable yet challenging trait for leaders wired as empaths is that they deeply experience the emotions, thoughts, and experiences of others. To distinguish from empathy, being empathetic incorporates understanding different points of view and being sensitive to people's emotions but not necessary feeling it in the body. Empaths listen deeply and understand people on an intuitive level, which allows them to detect emotions, feelings, thoughts, and their underlying truths. On the flip side, empaths struggle with being overwhelmed by other people's emotions if they unintentionally absorb other people's energies. If they don't establish healthy boundaries, they often experience fatigue, and, sometimes, become unable to be with large crowds for long periods of time. While being an empath can be a powerful gift, it also can be a curse. Empaths need to learn how to manage potential challenges to prevent emotional exhaustion and decision paralysis as a leader because they care so much about the well-being of people.

THE STRENGTHS OF EMPATHY IN THE WORKPLACE

In business, this often manifests in leaders who champion workplace inclusivity, mental health initiatives, and ethical decision-making. Empaths excel at creating psychologically safe environments where employees feel heard and valued. They can sense when a team member is struggling, without that person confiding in them, and they instinctively offer support. I worked with an executive in New Zealand, Edward, who exemplified these traits at work (as well as with his family and the refugees he helped).

Edward was able to read the emotional undercurrents in his leadership team. When a key executive was disengaged, he recognized the shift before any metrics reflected it, and, instead of being frustrated, he initiated a conversation to uncover the issue. By addressing this early and with the person's agreement to share it with the team, he retained a high performer and redistributed his work equitably, which improved the team's overall morale. The added benefit of this approach is that the team was extremely supportive of their teammate's tenacity in overcoming his challenge.

THE STRENGTHS OF EMPATHY IN THE FAMILY

With family whether at home or far away, empaths tend to be deeply attuned to their loved ones' emotions. They often sense stress or sadness before a word is spoken.

One day, Edward told me that his son was being bullied at school. "I know he's feeling stressed, but he's saying everything is fine," he said.

Out of curiosity, I asked, "Do you know what the cause of the bullying is?"

"Ever since he was very young, he loved wearing his mother's high heels, putting on lipstick, and wearing dresses. He went back and forth being a boy and girl. We thought it best to let him express his authentic self. But he is now fourteen and identifies as a girl. Our family accepts that, but there's pushback from the boys who mock him for wearing dresses and makeup and the girls, who are uncomfortable when he uses their bathroom. The teachers are doing their best to help the students understand and accept someone who is transgender, but that's a big hurdle and still carries many social stigmas in the minds not only of these children, but adults as well."

I suggested he provide a safe space for his child (and use whatever pro-
nouns the child prefers—she, her, they, them, theirs to acknowledge his
child's stress) and work to continue developing an even stronger bond based
on empathy and trust.

THE STRENGTHS OF EMPATHY IN SOCIETY

Empaths are often drawn to advocacy and social change because they feel
the struggles of others as if they were their own. Many of the most impactful
leaders in history—figures like Martin Luther King Jr. or Mother Teresa—
channeled their deep emotional sensitivity into movements that changed the
world.

For Edward that meant leading the charge to help Ukrainian refugees get
legal counsel from immigration lawyers so they could help hundreds flee to
countries in Europe. This was dear to his heart because his wife was Ukrainian. Her family lived in Kiev. He persuaded his company and his team to
support and contribute to the cost of providing legal assistance.

What's rather remarkable is that Edward leverages his empathic abilities
positively in all three areas of his life—at work, with family, and for a humanitarian cause. By the way, his number one value is love. Does that surprise you?

THE CHALLENGES OF EMPATHY IN THE WORKPLACE

While being empathic can be a core leadership advantage, it can become
a liability when taken to an extreme. Empaths often struggle with making
tough decisions because they feel the weight of how those choices impact
others. A senior executive I coached agonized over putting a team member
on a Professional Improvement Plan (PIP). His emotional investment in his
direct report made him delay the decision. He felt like a father figure to this
young man and wanted the best for him.

Unfortunately, his delay in acting diminished team morale because they consistently had to pick up the unfinished work of this young man. He also empathized with and cared about the rest of his team. He soon started to pick up on their frustration that resulted from this inequitable workload, which led to decreased work-life balance for his team due to an increase in hours worked per day.

Ultimately, he asked for help from Human Resources, and they guided him on how best to implement the PIP for this young man. The process anguished him, but learning to balance empathy with strategic decision-making is essential.

THE CHALLENGES OF EMPATHY IN THE FAMILY

Empaths sometimes struggle to set emotional boundaries with loved ones, taking on their stress as if it were their own. A recently married woman I coached described how she felt she needed to be there for everyone in her new family, which included four new kids, their school struggles, her partner's work stress, even her mother who had objected to the marriage for religious reasons. Until then, she had been living independently with no responsibilities other than herself, her job, and her immediate family who lived in another country. Being a good soldier, she jumped into "fixing" everyone's problems. The emotional burden left her exhausted and unable to care for herself.

We worked together on creating a "me-plan" for her mental, physical, and spiritual well-being. She chatted openly with her partner about this plan and he agreed. They then created a plan for their own happiness as a couple to keep their passionate flame alive. They agreed to work together to build their relationship with her mother, knowing it would take some time. Learning to support others in their time of need without absorbing their emotions or taking on their issues as your own is an indispensable skill for empaths in families and all interpersonal relationships.

THE CHALLENGES OF EMPATHY IN SOCIETY

Being deeply affected by societal issues can lead to chronic emotional, mental, psychological, and physical exhaustion, and, when extreme, burnout. Empaths often feel overwhelmed by other people's suffering wherever it occurs, making it difficult to stay enthusiastically engaged in work and life. For example, watching the news can cause anxiety, and trigger anger or sadness depending on what is being covered. I often suggest reading about or listening to the news instead of watching the unsettling images on the screen. This tactic lessens the empathic response of feeling deeply others' pain or anger over injustice.

An empathic human rights lawyer I worked with struggled to sustain her advocacy efforts because the weight of injustice became too much to bear. At times, she'd become so angry, she couldn't control her emotions, and she became known as a "loose cannon." When she learned of it, she understood that she had to learn how to channel her passion for human rights and social justice into sustainable action rather than the anger and emotional depletion because she felt so deeply her clients' frustrations, anger, and weariness from the injustices they experienced.

HARNESSING EMPATHY WITHOUT LOSING YOURSELF

If you are an empath—no matter where it occurs, work, family, or society—it's important to learn how to regulate your emotional engagement. Strategies like setting healthy boundaries, practicing self-care, and developing resilience are fundamental. If you work or live with an empath, understand their sensitive nature and accept the positive qualities they bring to the world and, if necessary, help them conquer the challenging aspects of their inherent nature to be stronger emotionally.

Empathy, when managed well, is a tremendous asset. But when unrestrained, it can become a burden. The challenge isn't in suppressing it; it's in learning how to use it wisely. Empaths who master this balance can inspire, connect, and drive change without losing themselves in the process.

TAKE 2: THE POWER AND PITFALLS OF SENSITIVITY

Some individuals can listen beyond people's words—they *feel* other people's energy as well as their own. It's not the same as empathy. It's a cool phenomenon. Is it linked to the quantum field whereby invisible fields interact with one another or, perhaps, even flow right through us?

For example, one client told me she can sense her colleagues' and family members' energy but can't pick up on their feelings. A bit like being tone deaf in music, where one can't distinguish between high or low notes or when singing one is unable to match the melody.

THE STRENGTHS OF SENSITIVITY IN THE WORKPLACE

Empathy and sensitivity are related but different. In brief, sensitivity relates to a person's heightened awareness to others and environmental stimuli while empathy refers to understanding different perspectives and feelings of others. For instance, Rafael, who often attended conferences for his international organization, was able to read a room as soon as he stepped into it. There could be twenty tables with ten people at each. He would prepare beforehand and choose the people he wanted to get to know; meaning those who would benefit his organization and/or develop his professional network. Almost every time, he'd end up sitting next to someone high profile without even knowing them. This person would have been on his list. He didn't know how he did it, but, time after time, it reinforced his trust in his ability to scan the energy of a room before choosing a particular seat at a particular table.

This leader was highly attuned to energy and could pick up on subtle dynamics, whether in a big conference room or at a team meeting. He leveraged this sensitivity trait into an advantage for strategic networking and detecting simmering conflicts before they'd escalate at team meetings. For example, seeing the bigger picture helped him while working on a cross-functional project being implemented by two separate teams. Both teams were utilizing resources separately to get to the same goal. He sensed growing frustration between the two departments, although it hadn't yet surfaced in meetings. This allowed him to address it early and prevent a major breakdown in collaboration. He was then able to steer them back on track and to communicate more frequently, share resources to improve cost efficiencies, and use AI tools to increase fifteenfold the speed without losing sight of quality. The two teams from two different departments might have gotten bogged down, but because he was able to read the room, he was instrumental in strengthening cross-functional collaboration and building an efficient organizational culture.

THE STRENGTHS OF SENSITIVITY
WITH FAMILY AND FRIENDS

At home, being sensitive to others' energies can strengthen relationships. Parents who sense their child's unspoken emotions can respond with compassion before the child even articulates their struggles or the reverse can also happen. A client once told me that it was his four-year old son who called him out for not being in tune with his own emotions.

His son said, "Daddy, you're hurting."

My client had been overwhelmed by personal issues. His son picked up on his father's emotions and feelings, which made my client realize that he had to work on becoming aware of his emotions and the energy that he was subconsciously emitting that, extraordinarily, was picked up on by his four-year-old son. You often learn and grow from your children.

In romantic relationships, sensitivity can foster deep connection—partners feel truly seen and understood. A spouse who recognizes when their partner is overwhelmed without needing words can offer support at the right moment—through a conversation, listening deeply and acknowledging what the partner is going through, or with a simple hug demonstrating that the other person has been seen and heard—and strengthen the relationship.

With friendships, this sensitivity to the other person's energy can translate into receiving a call when one friend is overloaded with work and having health issues, even without the friend in need telling the other who's thousands of miles apart or even continents apart.

THE STRENGTHS OF SENSITIVITY IN SOCIETY

Many social changemakers, spiritual leaders, and social justice advocates possess this sensitivity. They can feel the weight of collective emotions, for example, feeling the anxiety of a community facing injustice, human rights abuses, ongoing war, or even environmental problems. Leaders who use this awareness constructively can mobilize people toward healing and action. Think of great leaders like Nelson Mandela, Eleanor Roosevelt, the Dalai Lama, Martin Luther King Jr., Greta Thunberg, and Mala Yousafzai. They all addressed national and international crises not just with facts and policies, but, motivated by the emotional energy of a moment and acknowledging and conveying that energy to those around them, were able to harness that power and help others move through it. Their success lies in creating systemic change for the good of all.

THE CHALLENGES OF SENSITIVITY
IN THE WORKPLACE

The same ability that allows a leader to read a room can also drain them. Constantly feeling other people's stress, frustration, insecurities, or low energy can make it difficult to stay centered. Rafael, for example, after attending a conference during the day, felt emotionally, mentally, psychologically, and physically exhausted, not because of his workload, but because he absorbed all the unspoken anxieties of everyone in the room.

He dealt with it by declining all social activities in the evening, ordering room service, calling his wife and children, chilling out in his hotel room, and getting a good night's sleep to re-energize for the following day.

Introverts can feel this way, too, but Rafael was an extrovert and had to learn how to acknowledge the energy without carrying it or being controlled by it. Not an easy lesson to implement. Being self-aware and conscious of your and other people's energy enables you to take baby steps toward leveraging its strengths and diminishing its undesirable effects.

THE CHALLENGES OF SENSITIVITY IN THE FAMILY

In personal relationships, the biggest challenge is often emotional overabsorption. When you deeply feel a partner's stress, a child's sadness, or a parent's disappointment, it can be difficult to separate their emotions from your own. One client shared how, after visiting her aging father who was in the first stages of Alzheimer's, she would carry his disorientation for days. She would forget where she put her cell phone, have trouble finding words, and found herself repeating questions. She became alarmed because this was not her typical behavior.

I explained that she was not alone; other people also pick up on the vibrations of others. Understanding that it wasn't something wrong with her but rather that she had the innate ability to absorb others' emotions and energies was reassuring. With increased awareness and practice checking in on her energy and emotions by asking herself, "Is it me? Or is it coming from someone around me?" she became more adept with the process and realized after another visit to her parent's home, "Oh, it's not me. The energy is coming from my father." She was taking back control of her life.

Without clear boundaries, this kind of emotional entanglement can lead to fatigue, sadness, depression, worry, and anxiety. Often the highly sensitive individual, like my client, doesn't know where it's coming from until, for example, they receive a phone call from someone they know who shares how they've been battling depression and how they've finally sought help from a psychotherapist to improve their well-being.

THE CHALLENGES OF SENSITIVITY IN SOCIETY

Trying to save the world and feeling the weight of the world's challenges can be overwhelming. Many highly sensitive people struggle with a sense of helplessness when confronted with systemic issues, suffering, or collective fear. The human rights attorney I once coached was so deeply affected by the struggles of the communities she served that she experienced empathic and energetic burnout. She tried to learn how to stay engaged without carrying the world's problems on her shoulders. She couldn't do it as a social change agent. She let go and moved on to another profession in the corporate world that was less taxing and less draining.

BALANCING SENSITIVITY WITH STRENGTH

For those who feel a wide range of energies, the challenge isn't turning them off—it's learning how to manage them effectively. Some strategies include:

- **Setting energetic boundaries:** Recognizing what is yours to carry. Is it your karma or another's?
- **Practicing energetic resets:** Engaging in mindfulness, physical movement, healing, or time in nature to recalibrate.
- **Turning awareness into action:** Rather than being overwhelmed by what you feel, use it to make informed, purposeful choices.

Leaders who master this balance—who can sense the energy around them without being consumed by it—bring a rare and invaluable presence to their teams, their families, and society. Their ability to deeply connect, understand, and guide others is a strength, but only when they learn to protect their own energy in the process.

TAKE 3: INTUITION IN DECISION-MAKING

Intuition comes from the interaction of your rational process of thinking with innate knowing. It's often described as a hunch, a gut feeling, or a sudden Aha! moment. It is likely we all have experienced it and can remember those times whether we acted on a gut feeling or suppressed it depending on the context of the situation. Intuition can even emerge through the interpretation of dreams, which bring unconscious thoughts to light. Artists use it as inspiration. Think Salvador Dali. Scientists tap into intuition as a means of exploration. Think Albert Einstein. Leaders, too, rely on it when making decisions that align with their vision. Think Steve Jobs and Elon Musk.

There are many definitions of intuition. For the purpose of keeping in alignment through mindfulness, the Zen point of view is useful: Intuition can be developed through meditation, quieting the mind, becoming one with a higher intelligence, finding the patterns, connecting the dots, seeing the big picture in an empathetic way, and then knowing the answer or finding the ability to create through inner knowing, whether it's for yourself, your work, or for society. It's similar to heart-brain coherence—what you feel in your heart aligns with your thinking.

INTUITION IN THE WORKPLACE

A startup cofounder and CEO believed he could build a high-tech company based on his track record of optimizing operations, strengthening financials, and leading successful exits. He invited an angel investor to visit the company's headquarters, meet with other investors and board members, and consider participating in a seed funding round to provide further capital to refine a prototype and make sure the product aligns with customer needs and expectations before scaling.

The investor sensed discord—nothing specific—between management and the board as well as resistance from the other founder, the majority shareholder, toward implementing sustainable growth processes. She ignored her intuition and chose to invest. Early-stage investments, especially seed funding, always carry high risk. After a turbulent few years, the company came close to bankruptcy, and she resigned herself to the loss. In a retrospective analysis, she realized she had ignored her gut and decided that in the future she would focus on developing strategies that would help her recognize and trust her intuitive insights rather than dismissing them as irrational. It was a lesson that shaped her decision-making for life.

INTUITION AND SOCIAL POLICY

Planned Parenthood has a history of proactively responding to potential threats to the quality and affordability of reproductive healthcare access. For instance, in 2018, the organization collaborated with nearly eighty reproductive health, rights, and justice organizations to unveil the Blueprint aimed at transforming sexual and reproductive health policies in the United States and around the world.[1] This initiative was designed to anticipate and counteract legislative efforts that could restrict reproductive rights. These leaders combined logic, intuition, and forward thinking to create policies that would safeguard people's right to have autonomy over their bodies.

In essence, intuition is a powerful tool that bridges your rational mind with your innate wisdom. Whether it's in the form of a gut feeling, a dream interpretation, or a flash of insight, it guides you in personal and professional pursuits. By trusting and honing this inner wisdom, you can make decisions that resonate with your true purpose and vision.

TAKE 4: SHIFTING BELIEFS:
FLEXIBILITY AND TRANSFORMATION

It's sensible to be aware of your beliefs and to understand how some empower you while others can limit your growth, create walls, and hold you back from living your life in alignment with the energy you can get from excitement. The biggest question to ask when you're not in alignment with what excites you is, "What's stopping me?" Often, it's fear of the unknown. Sometimes it's a rational thought pitting your responsibility against taking a leap of faith to follow the rhythm of your inner voice.

To counter the fear, start with baby steps. Try out a new initiative or a passion project alongside your day-to-day job to determine if this new endeavor is the right one for you. You might decide to keep your job and carve out time outside work to spend on creative activities, nonprofit work, volunteering at your children's school as a board or committee member, or engage in sports to keep fit. If you're at a crossroads in your life, this is the time to dive deeper to see what would give you the meaning and fulfillment you haven't found in the daily grind of corporate life.

Beliefs are malleable. You can shift your perceptions by questioning yourself to increase self-awareness with the intention of unlocking new possibilities—personally, professionally, and in society. A client from China interpreted this as being "suspicious of herself" as a cross-check to keep her beliefs in alignment with her values.

SHIFTING BELIEFS IN THE WORKPLACE

Many new leaders of teams called people managers, especially high performers and former subject matter experts (SMEs), struggle with the belief that they can do everything faster by themselves than by delegating when it's urgent. They think that they have to personally handle every challenge to ensure success.

From "I Do It Better and Faster"
to "I Can Empower Others"

One executive I coached, instead of freeing up time for the strategic work he was meant to fulfill, which was a constant issue with his boss, felt overwhelmed because he believed delegating meant losing control. Over time, we worked to shift his mindset from seeing delegation as a risk to viewing it as an opportunity to empower and professionally develop his team. Once he started entrusting others with key projects, it reduced his stress and freed up his time to focus on strategic planning. His manager recognized how both he and his team grew in confidence, contributing increased business value to the organization.

From "Conflict Avoidance"
to "Conflict Can Lead to Opportunities"

A senior leader avoided difficult conversations because she disliked confrontation. This belief led to unresolved issues within her team, causing frustration and resistance when she was tasked with leading them to adopt an innovative, technological system that would make their work easier, faster, and more efficient. By reframing conflict as a growth opportunity to deepen understanding, engage with her team's ideas and concerns, and practice empathy while influencing without authority, her view of these crucial conversations shifted from conflict avoidance to curiosity. The result? Her once-resistant team eagerly embraced the technological innovations, inspired by her new communicative leadership approach.

SHIFTING BELIEFS IN THE FAMILY

As parents, the instinct to protect your children from pain and hardship is natural. However, shielding them too much can hinder their ability to think critically and solve problems on their own. Consider the metaphor of trees—wind and storms force them to extend their roots deep into the ground, providing the stability they need to grow tall and strong. Also, trees adapt to the winds by developing stress wood that prevents them from further harm. Without resistance, their roots remain shallow, and when the tree reaches a certain height, they collapse or aren't able to contort their positions to seek sunlight.[2] This phenomenon underscores the essential role of environmental stressors in natural development.

From "I Must Protect My Children" to "Challenges Help Them Grow"

Similarly, children need challenges to develop resilience, learn, and grow into capable, independent individuals. Just as trees require wind to build resilience, children need to face challenges to develop critical thinking and problem-solving skills. Overprotecting them can hinder their growth while stress increases their resilience and strength to face ups and downs throughout life.

I once coached a single, working mother who tried to protect her eleven-year-old son from cyberbullying by taking away his phone. While this solved one problem, it created another—his classmates teased him for not having a phone. Over time, she realized it's a balance between protecting him and supporting him when he faced challenges. Instead of overprotecting him or being a helicopter parent, she learned to step back and allow him to "strengthen his roots and stress wood" so he could support himself and grow more resilient mentally and psychologically at school, in sports, and, eventually, in a career or vocation.

If the problem might endanger her son, she was proactive and took action. For example, her son's soccer coach had a history of mistreating the boys, believing harshness would push them to win. Recognizing this situation was beyond her son's control, she rallied other parents to address the coach's behavior with the school principal.

Over time, by becoming more self-aware, she shifted her beliefs from fixing his problems to helping him develop the skills he needed to navigate them himself. One positive outcome was that he became more confident and capable. Another was that this new behavior transformed her relationship with him from one of dependency to interdependence, based on deeper respect and love. As a result, she felt lighter, less exhausted, and reassured by his newfound resilience.

SHIFTING BELIEFS AND SOCIETAL CHANGE

Volunteer for an organization where you're aligned with its mission to make a positive impact on its community. You may think, "I can't make a difference." But you may be surprised when you offer your skill set combined with your passion for a particular social cause. It's not impossible that leadership notices your impact as a change catalyst and asks you to keep contributing and invites you to play a bigger role. You're honored and realize that your small actions can create positive outcomes. Hence, you reframed your old belief to this new one, "I can make a difference," and it feels good.

From "I Can't Make a Difference"
to "Small Actions Create Positive Change"

A financial executive, Lisa, wanted more purpose in her life. At first, she wanted to create a rescue shelter for animals, but building it would take too much time. Instead, she volunteered with a local foundation fighting for the "Most Vulnerable People (MVP)" around the world—the Tim Tebow Foundation.[3] It's a Christian organization rooted in the values of faith, hope, and love. Their mission serves marginalized people in over ninety countries. Such initiatives give credence to the transformative power of love, compassion, and action.

Lisa volunteered for the "Night to Shine," which is a prom night experience for teens with special needs under the umbrella of Tebow's Special Needs

Ministry. Special needs include low-functioning neurodiverse individuals and those with cerebral palsy, down syndrome, bipolar disorder, visual impairment, and more. Since prom night is a fairytale experience for these adolescents, it's an escape from challenges and an experience of joy. Lisa recounted how every single teen experienced a red carpet entrance as a guest of honor, and that, later in the evening, they're crowned a king or queen. Beyond fun, Night to Shine celebrates the value, dignity, and inherent potential of these special needs teenagers.[4] Lisa emailed me about the experience. She concluded with, "I left the event feeling uplifted and grateful for the new friendships I had formed." What a beautiful experience to volunteer for a cause that you believe in and that you find deeply fulfilling. This has become a yearly event globally empowering these individuals with self-worth and confidence.

Lisa's championing of these kids led to the executive director of the local chapter to offer her a full-time position. Lisa was honored, but chose to stay in her current position, where she is really happy, while continuing to volunteer yearly for the Night to Shine prom event. Someday she may change her mind if circumstances at her current job change. For now, Lisa moved from "I can't make a difference" to "I can take small actions to create positive change."

From "People Are Either Good or Bad" to "People Are Complex and Capable of Change"

Polarized thinking leads to division. In today's world, many of us are quick to judge others based on a single action or belief. One of the most powerful shifts we can make as a society is to move away from rigid categorization and toward understanding human complexity. When we allow space for people to evolve, we create room for reconciliation, growth, and collective progress.

A client who changed his perception about a very controversial politician and businessman provides what to me is a profound example. A sales executive who voted against Trump reflected on how he could shift his negative beliefs about Trump. He dug deep within his psyche. He reasoned that there must be some inherent good in Trump that could resonate with something in him that would allow him to accept Trump as the 47th president. He came up with resilience. If you think about it, Trump is arguably one of the most resilient men on the planet, a strength both men shared.

By shifting his thinking to a Buddha-like enlightened mindset, my client was able to detach his emotions, respectfully disagree, and realize people are full of paradoxes. There is probably at least one trait or characteristic that you can identify with in another person that would help you understand him or her and allow you to bypass polarization of thought and action and seek cooperation, collaboration, and peace depending on the context.

SHIFTING BELIEFS FOR PERSONAL AND PROFESSIONAL GROWTH

Shifting beliefs isn't about forcing yourself to have or fake a positive attitude or ignoring reality. It's about examining the stories you tell yourself and asking:

- Is this belief serving me, or is it holding me back?
- What if I looked at this situation through a different lens?
- What new possibilities emerge if I choose a different belief?

When you consciously shift your beliefs in a positive direction as so many of my clients have, you open the door to transformation—not just for yourself, but for those around you. Whether in your family, at work, or in societal endeavors, the "intending good" beliefs you choose to hold, shape the world you create.[5]

TAKE 5: FORGING SELF-LOVE AND SELF-FORGIVENESS

Learning how to accept, love, and forgive yourself is an essential part of life's journey. One of my clients, a CEO from Canada, confided that "self-love and self-forgiveness is something I'm not sure I can do." He grew up in a Catholic setting and was abused as a boy by men hiding behind the vestments. As he matured, he realized he loved men, something he, like so many others at the time, believed had to be hidden until they had the courage to come out to their parents and others. This made him feel shame, guilt, social anxiety, which eventually led him to years of psychotherapy.

Where to start with self-love? It usually starts when you are older and more aware of yourself as a person. When I work with clients who are very self-critical, I ask them how they would treat their best friend or a colleague in a similar situation. They almost always say, "I give them grace, but I don't give myself grace." Being hard on oneself comes from many causes, including childhoods where they felt they had to be perfect and high performers. At work, it's excellent to be a high performer but not if it hinders or delays progress. Remember the saying, often attributed to Winston Churchill, "Perfection is the enemy of progress."

The next question I ask is, "How can you give yourself grace (self-compassion)?" Each person has their own unique responses. One reads a note a boss sent her praising her performance; another keeps a mug, given to her by colleagues, on her desk that reads, "You're crushing it." Both use these healthy rituals as reminders to nurture self-love. A surgeon's wife, when he's down because a procedure did not go well, brings out notebooks full of notes from his patients expressing their gratitude for his services. He's a very caring and empathetic surgeon and his wife reminds him to give himself grace.

Self-love means you accept yourself—your strengths and flaws—without judgment, by giving yourself grace. No one is perfect. Learn to treat yourself with kindness and respect. I heard once someone say, "Give yourself a permission slip." I suppose this goes back to guilt. Letting go of guilt, giving yourself a permission slip to treat yourself with dignity, is rather freeing. It helps you overcome your inner critic and make it your ally. Doing so will help you take care of yourself, improve your self-esteem and well-being, and lead you to healthier relationships personally and professionally. I received this note from a former client the other day: "This year I'm focused on being kinder to myself. I'm empowered to do this. No one else is responsible for my attitude and outlook each day. I'm staying true to me," a powerful testament to her practice of self-love.

There is scientific evidence that self-love has a positive impact on a person's overall satisfaction with life. It's not selfish. It is necessary to take care of your needs and to work toward self-actualization, meaning among many things that you don't need to sacrifice your needs for the career of your partner, the ambitions of your boss, or pleasing others to keep the peace. It is not selfish but rather necessary for your well-being. Evidence-shows that self-love contributes to "better mental health, more self-acceptance, higher self-esteem, more motivation, stronger determination, increased self-awareness, less anxiety, and better sleep."[6]

Self-reflection plays a big part in developing self-love. You can learn from your mistakes. When something doesn't work out the way you wanted it to, reflect on the reasons why it didn't. Journaling, meditation, talking it over with a trusted partner or a colleague (depending on the context) are good ways to do it. You can push yourself hard but push with the strength that comes from nurturing and self-love. Leadership from the heart inspires people to be better versions of themselves.

What role does self-forgiveness play in life's theatrical drama? It builds upon the false belief that you have to be hard on yourself to be successful or a perfectionist to be a high performer. It relates to self-judgment, allowing your inner critic to say harsh things about you to prevent incompetence which originated in early humans as a survival instinct, and has evolved to this day through religious and cultural beliefs and practices.[7] Evidence-based research shows that self-forgiveness, like self-love, leads to increased well-being, a positive attitude, healthier relationships, and success.

It's about being okay after making a mistake, learning to overcome challenges that, if you let them, can increase your resilience, and creating healthy expectations of yourself. Forgiving yourself will help you to limit stress, anxiety, and disappointment. To achieve this, go back to your values—your foundational roots—to empower you to be kind to yourself, understanding, compassionate, loving, and forgiving. Self-forgiveness, like self-love, is a practice. Take baby steps. Get back up when you fall down. Learn and grow from your mistakes, give yourself grace, and be grateful for the life you have, and know others need you.

TAKE 6: PLEASING PEOPLE:
SELFISH OR ALTRUISTIC?

A people pleaser is someone who tends to prioritize others' needs before their own. The cause may stem from, among other things, childhood experiences. Although I'm not a psychologist, based on my experience coaching people pleasers, I've found it is often linked to parents who emotionally manipulate their children to meet the parents' needs first, often by rejecting or ignoring them. To feel accepted, loved, acknowledged, and valued, the child learns to please the parent first, and this habit is later transferred to pleasing others. The person gives to feel safe or liked, not out of generosity. The price they pay is high. It comes at the expense of living their own life in a meaningful way. Self-awareness can help them take measures to change this behavior. Depending on how deep-rooted it is, self-help books, psychotherapy, and even coaching can help.

There is a flip side. Some people pleasers are genuinely driven by self-expression.[8] This is a desire to share with others without the need for reciprocity. People like this often donate their time and money to nonprofits and causes to benefit humanity. They intend good and it feels good.

There is a fine line between people pleasers you don't want to enable because it perpetuates an unhealthy situation and those who give without an ulterior motive. Discerning the difference is tricky. Allow others who give to you in good faith to do so. It helps them to give, and it is good for you to receive their gift with unconditional love. However, if you sense the person is giving *only* to be loved or accepted rather than a genuine desire to please you, then graciously tell the person you appreciate them for who they are, not what they give you. Doing so validates their self-worth and strengthens your own sense of fulfillment as a healthy receiver. Healthy relationships are based on a balance between give and take and being with others who like or love you for who you are and those looking to be loved and accepted by you.

If you are a people pleaser, who once gave only to please, but have now become self-aware and changed, and the people you've been pleasing reject you because you're no longer giving to please, then it's a gift to move on, and be with people who resonate with your new behavior. It's better to live in alignment with your own needs and wants, not narcissistically, but truthfully in sync with your values and your authentic self. You can still help others but now you do it for positive reasons, not because you want them to like you. Being true to yourself improves healthy relationships personally and professionally.

If you are or aren't a people pleaser, think about a time you stood up for yourself. What were the consequences? Did living your life with integrity aligned with your values increase your self-esteem?

TAKE 7: REDEFINING THE IMPOSTER SYNDROME

What surprises me most about the imposter syndrome is that it comes up with both men and women regardless of race, age, hierarchical position, profession, or industry. A quick Google search defines imposter syndrome as "the persistent inability to believe that one's success is deserved or has been legitimately achieved as a result of one's own efforts or skills."[9] Imposter syndrome comes from the belief that you are a fraud, you are just lucky, and that others overestimate your abilities. People with imposter syndrome may feel they must take every certification beyond those that are required in their field because they are not smart enough and feel the need to prove themselves through excessive effort. These "imposters" often fear failure, doubt their abilities, or dread being found out as not deserving their position or promotion in spite of the evidence of competence and a proven track record. Despite these feelings, these professionals are at the top of their game, high performers, and excellent leaders.

My first encounter with someone with imposter syndrome was with a brilliant executive working at an international organization in Geneva, Switzerland. He kept saying, "I'm lucky. I've always been lucky with my career."

According to a Korn Ferry survey of 400 executives, 71 percent of CEOs and 65 percent of senior executives have experienced or exhibited signs of imposter syndrome.[10] Korn Ferry described this as a "crisis of confidence" for 85 percent of these leaders who paradoxically expressed their capability, competence, and success as evidenced by their job performance. On the contrary, John Rau warns against pathologizing it, and says, based on his experience, "This feeling is not a bug, but rather a *feature* of what people stepping into the CEO role feel."[11]

Based on my primary research, I believe it is to the result of beliefs and feelings that disappear once the person grows more comfortable in their new position or role. When you step into new roles, especially as a CEO or part of the C-Suite, or as a senior executive, it's normal to not know everything. You become responsible for making decisions that evolve from futures scenario planning three to five years ahead. In the military, planning extends even further, sometimes fifty years into the future. Given this level of ambiguity, it's natural for leaders to temporarily feel self-doubt that diminishes as unknowns become known and they gain clarity or they reframe their fear of the unknown into the feeling of excitement. In either case, the feeling they are an imposter evaporates.

In this context, experiencing a crisis of confidence isn't a weakness; it reflects humility and a healthy leadership mindset. Conversely, leaders who claim to have all the answers from the outset are likely setting themselves up for failure. Perhaps it's time to redefine imposter syndrome. This perspective aligns with emerging research that challenges traditional views on imposter syndrome.

MIT Sloan professor Basima Tewfik has written, "It's time to rethink some of our old ideas about impostorism."[12] She prefers the phrase "imposter thoughts at work," but I've found that some of my clients even feel the imposter syndrome in other roles, for example, as parents. They believe they are not measuring up as a mother or father; they can never meet their own high standards, even when they receive praise from their parents and friends telling them that they're amazing with their children.

I prefer looking at one's life holistically, and strategies can be applied for this phenomenon personally and professionally. Tewfik debunked four myths, but I'll focus only on the first: Myth 1: the "imposter phenomenon is permanent."[13] This corroborates my research demonstrating that the belief can change based on the context and even lines up with Buddha's law of impermanence—everything in the universe is in a constant state of change.

Workplaces and society can support individuals experiencing thoughts of imposterism by helping them understand that these feelings are neither good nor bad and that they can be managed with practical strategies, tools, and guidance. If you feel this way, it is important to know that navigating your feelings isn't something you have to do alone. Seeking support can make a meaningful difference. It's okay for you to feel discomfort and work through it, together with a trusted partner, confidante, colleague, friend, mentor, or spiritual advisor. The initial step takes courage. It involves opening yourself up and sharing your self-doubts with trustworthy individuals in your life who are supportive, unbiased, and nonjudgmental, people who can offer honest feedback and help you reframe imposter thoughts into a more empowering view of your intelligence and capabilities. The goal is to move past imposterism so it no longer holds you back. Some quick tips: Trust yourself, know you're valued, limit negative self-talk, avoid comparing yourself to others, remember that just because it happened in the past doesn't mean it's going to happen in the present, focus on becoming comfortable with uncertainty, and reframe fear of the unknown to excitement.

Ultimately, you want to prevent imposterism from negatively impacting your life. According to Susan David, PhD, a psychologist at Harvard Medical School, "When people buy into impostor stories and treat them as fact, it can stop people from putting themselves out there, taking risks, or moving forward. It can prevent people from living life in ways that are congruent with their values."[14] I wholeheartedly agree.

Finally, imposter syndrome doesn't disappear overnight, but with intentional strategies, you can learn to manage it rather than be controlled by it. By shifting your mindset, embracing growth, and leveraging support networks, you can step into your personal and professional roles with greater confidence and authenticity. It's not about eliminating all self-doubt, but for you to recognize it, challenge it, and move forward with resourcefulness, practicality, and gumption.

TAKE 8: TAPPING INTO YOUR INNER CHILD

Why in the world is this important? You may have different values, but many of my clients emphasize that their life has to be fun, playful, and interesting both at work and in their personal lives. One client in FinTech told me, "Fun used to be a value at our company. After the pandemic, the fun disappeared." He addressed it with those above him, and they have reinstated it. A CEO/executive director of an educational organization told me, "Life and work have to be fun, playful, and interesting." Both men have kept their inner child alive and were able to bring it into their personal and professional lives.

For some, taking life seriously means forgetting about their inner child, which is characterized by enthusiasm, zest for life, and curiosity. As adults, these qualities can be lost because we become like a hamster on a treadmill, caught up in the rat race, striving to be high performers and climb the leadership ladder toward our desires. If you have children, these feelings may come alive as you experience childhood's pleasures with them, and your inner child's sense of awe and wonder reemerges. When is the last time you experienced awe and wonder?

There are other ways to wake your inner child. For example, imagine you're meeting your younger self. You could be five or a teenager. Where would it be? What are you doing? How does it make you feel? You might want to ask your younger self what it wants from you. Does it want you to let yourself play and have fun? Answer by giving your adult self permission to enjoy life at the same time as you are working diligently toward your goals and aspirations. You can create your own awesome story. Allow your imagination to come alive. Keeping your inner child alive helps you not take life too seriously, but instead allows you to play the game of life with pleasure. Taking actions based on how the energy of excitement leads you toward self-realization.

Having conversations like this opens you up to possibilities and opportunities. At times, you're hit with a curveball in life: For instance, your company is going through a massive reorg and you are going to be laid off, albeit with a package. That's when your inner child reassuringly jumps in and nudges you to think positively about people transforming themselves, which allows you to explore a new path with a beginner's mind or Zen outlook. During one meeting, a client undergoing an existential change in his life, philosophically and with childlike wonder, shared these quotes with me:

"Once I stopped worrying about my career, my career took off."
—Doug Parker, former CEO of American Airlines[15]

"I stop thinking, start feeling. My shots become a half-second quicker, my decisions become the product of instinct rather than logic."
—Andre Agassi, who won a career Grand Slam for all four tennis singles major championships[16]

His shift was about tapping into a deeper, instinctive part of himself, the inner child that plays freely, trusts its gut, and acts without overthinking. By aligning with his core values rather than chasing perfection, he let intuition, not reasoning, guide his game.

My client knew he could embrace their perspectives, and they would help him transform his life to one that was even better. Both Parker and Agassi let go of their worries concerning maintaining images, which were not serving them well. Both men's careers soared to the highest peaks imaginable in their fields. Their inner child, I imagine, rejoiced because they were leading their lives from the inside out. My client followed suit.

There's a deeper psychological dimension to the inner child, but my focus here is simple: Reconnect with the joy, spontaneity, and the adventure of childlike qualities. By embracing that energy, you cultivate a healthier relationship with yourself and those around you. Your inner child invites you to play, while your adult self gives you reassurance and care—whether through meditation, reflection, telepathy, or self-compassion. This balance isn't just healing; it's a path to greater well-being and a more fulfilling life.

TAKE 9: UPGRADING YOUR EQ: YOUR BEST SELF

IQ and technical skills are relevant, but if you want to be in a leadership role, emotional intelligence (EQ) is a crucial skill and can be learned. Daniel Goleman helped popularize this term coined by researchers John Mayer and Peter Salovey in 1990.[17] EQ helps you become self-aware, which helps you manage your emotions, stay calm during difficult conversations, avert crises proactively, effectively solve problems, and treat your colleagues with love, empathy, and compassion. You can incorporate these skills into your social intelligence (SQ), which proves important for leading teams and collaborating cross-functionally, because by actively listening you understand their perspective.[18] It is also effective when dealing with your spheres of influence. Leaders who cultivate EQ drive higher team performance, create stronger workplace cultures, and enhance business outcomes. Yet, despite the evidence, many leaders still underestimate the power of EQ and SQ, dismissing them as soft skills rather than business values.

Leaders with lower emotional intelligence often react impulsively, shut people out when frustrated, and deny how emotions influence their decisions. They defend rather than actively listen and often miss the subtle signals that indicate tension in a room. Leaders with higher emotional intelligence take a different approach. They speak calmly with intention, keep an open dialogue despite the pressure, and welcome feedback to ensure positive outcomes. They show genuine care for colleagues and are attuned to the unspoken moods and dynamics that shape the team environment.

If you are someone who gets triggered emotionally, reacts in angry outbursts, replies dismissively, or blames others, you have low EQ, but you can improve it with practice. See SmartTalentEQ's diagram (Figure Take 9.1), which illustrates the difference between a low and high EQ.[19]

FIGURE TAKE 9.1

Painting EQ's Complexity into Simplicity

Leaders with Low EQ . . .	Leaders with High EQ . . .
. . . sound off even when it won't help.	. . . only speak out when doing it helps the situation.
. . . brush people off when bothered.	. . . keep lines of communication open even when frustrated.
. . . deny that emotions impact their thinking.	. . . recognize when other people are affecting their emotional state.
. . . get defensive when challenged.	. . . are open to feedback.
. . . focus only on tasks and ignore the person.	. . . show others they care about them.
. . . are oblivious to unspoken tension.	. . . accurately pick up on the mood of a room.

Source: Maggie Sass, "What a High Emotional Intelligence Looks Like," TalentSmartEQ, August 11, 2025, https://www.talentsmarteq.com/what-a-high-emotional -intelligence-looks-like/. Original chart model courtesy of Travis Bradberry.

I've seen many clients increase their EQ with dedicated practice and their peers and bosses noticed, which gave them a sense of pride and satisfaction and motivated them to keep growing their EQ and leadership skills. One client who achieved a higher EQ with mindful practice brought together four teams from Asia, Australia, and South and North America to collaborate in parallel on a project that got done in three weeks rather than the projected three months. He did it by actively listening to their concerns and ideas, understanding their strengths and weaknesses, empowering them with solutioning, and being empathetic to the varying time zones and their values regarding work-life balance. It turned out to be a win-win for all stakeholders.

I created an eight-week EQ plan as an action experiment with a client. He worked hard on developing his self-awareness and self-management—regulating his emotions during stressful scenarios, social awareness—as well as practicing empathy with his colleagues and managing relationships—effectively communicating and resolving conflict. His dedication created an engaged, productive, and resilient team based on his newfound high-trust team culture delivering business value, essentially by increasing revenue growth. His new mindset led to respect and collaboration, and he steered his team using an adaptive leadership style. The components of EQ equipped him to navigate today's workplace complexity and global connectivity. His inner work positively changed him. At the end of our coaching journey, he told me, "I've been transformed!"

There are skeptics who believe IQ and competence are enough and that business leaders are valued for their knowledge, expertise, and experience. These characteristics are a part of the equation, but, without EQ, technical ability doesn't translate into effective leadership. Without EQ, leaders struggle to motivate, inspire, and rally their teams. If they are not self-aware and can't manage their emotions and behaviors or build trustworthy relationships, it'll be a challenge to inspire followership, commitment, team engagement, and a thriving high-trust high-performing culture within the organization. Which kind of leader do you want to be? One who has a command-and-control style of leadership with a low EQ? Or one who inspires others to be the best versions of themselves and contributes value to their organization with a high EQ?

Strengthening your EQ is a leadership advantage. It's not innate but a skill you can develop. Leaders who actively invest in self-awareness, self-management, social awareness, and relationship management will find themselves better equipped to lead in the face of uncertainty, complexity, and constant change. The most effective executives recognize that EQ is not a soft skill—it is the foundation of impactful leadership. According to TalentSmartEQ's research, "A leader's emotional intelligence (EQ) is so critical that it is responsible for 58 percent of his or her job performance. Likewise, more than 90 percent of top performers in leadership positions possess a high degree of EQ."[20] TalentSmartEQ's research further highlighted that high EQ people made more money, had better relationships, and lived happier and healthier lives in the workplace than those didn't.[21] EQ can improve all aspects of your life.

As illustrated in Figure Take 9.2, emotional intelligence is built on two core capacities: personal competence and social competence.[22] Personal

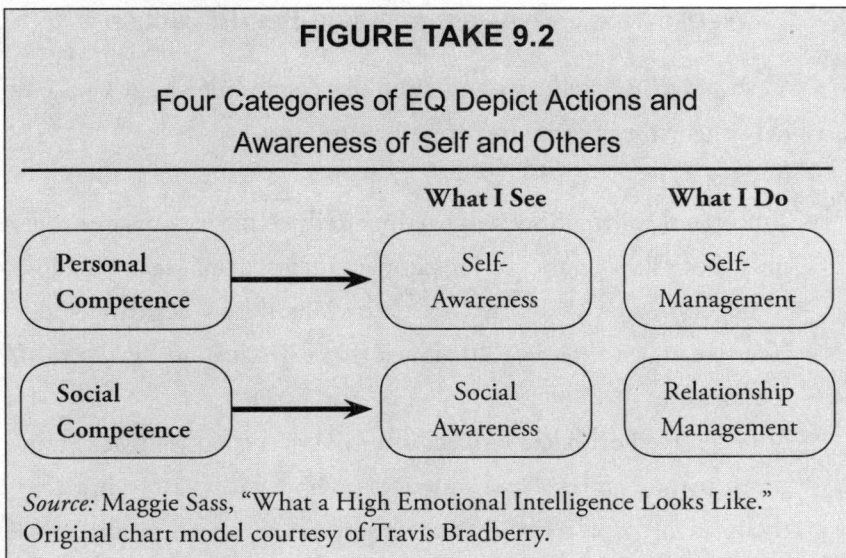

FIGURE TAKE 9.2

Four Categories of EQ Depict Actions and Awareness of Self and Others

	What I See	What I Do
Personal Competence →	Self-Awareness	Self-Management
Social Competence →	Social Awareness	Relationship Management

Source: Maggie Sass, "What a High Emotional Intelligence Looks Like." Original chart model courtesy of Travis Bradberry.

competence involves self-awareness, recognizing your own emotions as they arise combined with self-management, which is the ability to respond to those emotions in ways that align with your values and goals. Social competence focuses on understanding others through social awareness, the skill of accurately reading the emotions and dynamics around you, and relationship management, which is the ability to use that insight to build trust, navigate conflict, and strengthen connections. Together, these four skills form the foundation for leading with clarity, empathy, and influence.

By mastering EQ, you enrich interpersonal relationships personally, professionally, and socially. What follows is the ten-week plan that I've used with some clients. Try it as your own action experiment to strengthen your EQ and SQ skills. It's a starting point to gain self-awareness and empathy for others, which is the foundation for building EQ. It's also a tool for strengthening your effective leadership skills by enhancing your people management skills.

EQ AND SQ TEN-WEEK PLAN

Weeks 1–2: Self-Awareness and Self-Reflection

- **Goal:** Build deeper self-awareness and understanding about your emotional triggers, strengths, and areas for growth.
- **Activities:**
  - **Emotional Journal:** Start journaling daily to develop awareness about how your emotions impact interpersonal relationships. Reflect on why you felt that way, especially if it's a negative emotion like anger, then work to adjust those strong emotions in future interactions.
  - **360-Degree Feedback:** Collect informal or formal feedback from peers, team members, and superiors on how your actions impact them. Identify patterns in their responses and how they align with your self-perception.

○ **Weekly Reflection**: Each week, spend an hour reviewing your entries and the feedback you received, noting any key words, patterns, and surprises.

Weeks 3–4: Self-Management and Managing Stress

- **Goal**: Practice techniques to regulate emotions, especially in high-stakes situations, to maintain composure and decision-making ability.
- **Activities**:
  ○ **Mindfulness Practice**: Dedicate 1-15-30-60 minutes daily to mindfulness exercises (like focused breathing or meditation) to improve emotional regulation.
  ○ **Response Techniques**: Practice pausing before reacting, particularly during tense meetings or challenging conversations. Ask clarifying questions to give yourself time to process and understand the intent of the other person's feedback.
  ○ **Stress Management Plan**: Identify your top stressors and develop personalized strategies (e.g., prioritizing, delegating, taking short breaks, taking a sip of water, and breathing deeply) to address them proactively.

Weeks 5–6: Relationship Management and Empathy

- **Goal**: Develop empathy and enhance your listening skills to better understand your team and colleagues to build stronger relationships.
- **Activities**:
  ○ **Active Listening Exercise**: In conversations, focus on listening without planning your response. Aim to paraphrase the other person's words to ensure your understanding of what they're saying. Use nonverbal cues like tilting your head slightly or nodding your head up and down to give the other person the sense you're engaged. Focus on the conversation and avoid distractions—turn off notifications.

- **Team Check-Ins:** Set aside dedicated time each week for a team huddle, encourage your team to discuss both work and nonwork challenges impacting them.
- **Perspective-Taking:** Before giving feedback or making decisions, take a moment to consider the situation from others' perspectives and emotional states.

Weeks 7–8: Social Awareness and Influence

- **Goal:** Strengthen your networking, social, and influence skills to build rapport and alignment across departments and with key stakeholders.
- **Activities:**
  - **Network Expansion:** Schedule time to connect with leaders across departments. Approach these conversations with curiosity and a willingness to learn about their challenges and priorities. Adopt the Zen Buddhist mind, letting go of assumptions and being open to their perspectives.
  - **Influence Skills:** Start with low-stakes situations in which to practice influencing others by focusing on common goals, clear communication, and finding mutually beneficial solutions.
  - **Collaborative Mindset:** In team settings, encourage collaborative discussions and solutions, allowing others to feel emotional ownership of projects and decisions.

Ongoing Weekly Accountability and Review

- **Goal:** Iteration from feedback.
- **Activities:**
  - **Accountability Partner:** Find a partner, mentor, coach, or peer who can check in weekly to discuss your progress, challenges, and growth.

- ○ **Review and Adjust**: At the end of each week, assess your progress, make any necessary adjustments, and celebrate small wins to stay motivated.

Week 9–10: EQ, SQ, and Leadership Reflection

- **Goal**: Cultivating kindness in family, work, and society.
- **Activities**:
  - ○ **Reflect on your journey over these past eight weeks**: How you have grown, lessons learned, and how you are progressing toward your EQ, SQ, empathy, and leadership aspirations?
  - ○ Identify key growth areas to continue developing on an ongoing basis.

This approach builds on incremental growth in the core competencies of EQ and SQ, helping you improve your soft skills while creating a better you from the inside out. Based on experience, people in your family, workplace, and social circles are going to notice your transformation. It's time to lead yourself, others, and organizations with the power of EQ and SQ!

TAKE 10: LEADING WITH SOCIAL INTELLIGENCE

Social intelligence (SQ) builds upon one of the four EQ competencies—social awareness. It focuses on understanding and responding to others. EQ's foundation relies upon self-awareness and self-management, including emotional regulation. Many organizations consider both EQ and SQ important leadership skills that empower leaders to navigate complex relationships, facilitate collaboration, and create a high-performing culture.

What's the difference between leadership and management? Leaders envision and guide change through influence while management executes, coordinating people to implement processes and maintain systems in alignment with organizational goals. Both focus on people; therefore, SQ is important for everyone in an organization. You can be a leader regardless of your title and position if you inspire, motivate, influence, align, encourage, and empower others, including external stakeholders, to take action whether up, down, or across the organizational structure. SQ helps shape your leadership skills.

You can start by being a role model, leading by example. Many clients are commended in their performance reports with having this ability to intrinsically inspire themselves and others to align their team's goals with the company's vision and mission of driving change and innovation. These leaders are perceived as positive, confident, open to learning and growing, transparent in their communication style, decisive yet empathetic, humble, and appreciative of the people they work with—in alignment with the humancentric approach—treating colleagues with respect and dignity.

EQ and SQ didn't come easily to them. They put in the effort, learned from feedback, practiced, reiterated, progressed, and, eventually, were recognized and acknowledged by their direct reports, peers, and senior leaders as someone they "loved to work with" and were "looking forward to future collaborations" with, and were "impressed with your innovative drive leading and leveraging AI tools to improve efficiencies" for the company. I could cite more accolades, but these give you the picture of the power of the soft skills.

Soft power contributes toward meaningful human connection. A people-first approach is the support structure for an engaged workplace culture. Employees today need to focus on purpose and belonging while leveraging technology and AI as tools for increased productivity, which can lead to a feeling of isolation. Even introverts need social connection, especially when working remotely. One client went to the nearest office for one day per month, worked on-site, and socialized with whomever was there that day, which may have required meeting new colleagues. It was outside of his comfort zone, but he did it. Afterwards, he felt happier and his sense of well-being improved. Quarterly, he brought his team, who all worked remotely, together for a three-day off-site that was somewhere in the middle of their geographic zones, and he did it within budget. This improved team morale and joy, and created connection, resulting in a supportive environment conducive to higher performance. His social engagement strategies worked for himself and his team. Organizational environments are unique, which means every leader can address the needs of their team members by being inclusive when building an effective culture that adapts to changing times, ensures respect, motivates, and supports well-being and long-term success.

Developing social intelligence is an ongoing process that requires practice, feedback, and reflection. Leaders who invest in this skill create human-centric cultures centered on empathy, build agile teams, inspire, influence, and align people toward innovative change, and become positive role models for others to emulate and follow on their own leadership pathways, enhancing the leadership pipeline within organizations.

Here are some skills you need to improve your social intelligence. If you have them all, or some of them, fine. If you know someone who can benefit from understanding some of these abilities, please share these insights with them so we can, together, cultivate a more empathetic world.

ESSENTIAL SQ SKILLS AND ABILITIES

1. **Reading the Room:** Strong leaders can pick up on verbal and nonverbal cues and recognize underlying emotions, group dynamics, and unspoken concerns. This awareness allows them to adjust their approach in real time. Empaths are particularly adept at this skill.

2. **Building Trust and Rapport:** Leaders with high social intelligence nurture psychological safety, making it easier for teams to communicate openly, share ideas, and take risks. Trust is built through consistent actions, transparency, and empathy.

3. **Navigating Difficult Conversations:** Whether giving feedback, resolving conflicts, or managing resistance to change, socially intelligent leaders approach difficult discussions with empathy and clarity. They balance assertiveness with understanding. They have no need for

abrasive tactics, such as yelling, employing the stick-and-carrot method, and acting in an authoritarian command-and-control style of leadership to effectively manage teams.

4. **Influencing and Persuading**: Effective leaders know how to align multiple perspectives, diversity of thought, and to inspire commitment, and gain buy-in without relying on authoritarian hierarchical power. They target their messaging to resonate with different audiences and key stakeholders.

5. **Creating Cultural and Situational Awareness**: Social intelligence requires adapting leadership styles to the organizational culture, team dynamics, and individual personalities. What works in one context may not work in another.

6. **Leading with Empathy**: Understanding the needs, motivations, and challenges of team members allows leaders to provide meaningful support and increase engagement and retention.

Building upon emotional intelligence with social skills improves human interactions. You need a village to achieve success that requires collaboration, communication, and alignment toward bold goals. Keep an open mind and keep honing your leadership capabilities. The world needs more leaders with emotional and social intelligence to unleash even greater potential in people, empowering them to do their best work and create a more humane environment in which everyone thrives.

In an era dominated by Tech and AI, people need human connection. One client, a VP of engineering, recently predicted that AI could improve a hundredfold and reduce costs by 15 percent within eighteen months. What used to take him two days to research now takes just two minutes, thanks to the right framework and prompts. Of course, he reviews and checks the results for accuracy. When I asked him what he planned to do with all his extra time, he said it's an opportunity to network, explore new opportunities, and mentor junior staff. As a social species, we are entering a new era where technology and AI can free you to build deeper connections—something many of us crave after being isolated behind screens for so long. The future is not one of isolation, but one of profound human connection, driven by the power of technology and emotional and social intelligence.

In essence, leadership, emotional intelligence, social intelligence, and AI don't have to be at odds but can complement each other. As AI enhances efficiency, reduces costs, and takes over more routine tasks, you can focus more on the human aspects of your role: connection, empathy, and development of mental, emotional, physical, social, and spiritual well-being. This could lead to more empowered, engaged teams, and, ultimately, a more humane work culture founded on the values of respect and dignity. These technological advancements are opportunities rather than threats. With this perspective, are you ready to prioritize human relationships and leadership that nurtures those connections in ways technology never could?

While AI offers new possibilities, it also introduces challenges that cannot be ignored. Another wise client, a tech lead from an innovative company in Cambridge, England, pointed out the risks. During a recent conversation, she shared the flip side, "AI is improving at an incredible pace month by month," she acknowledged, "but it comes with risks." She mentioned as examples that leaders may prioritize data-driven recommendations over intuitive, human-centered decision-making, thereby weakening trust and authentic relationships between leaders and their teams.

Shifting gears, her voice taking on a more personal note, she added, "The other night, my eleven-year-old nephew got caught by his mom, still awake at 4 a.m., glued to his screen, watching his favorite AI-generated musician. They finally understood why he was exhausted at school." She shook her head. Some of my clients who are parents of children around the same age were trying to manage situations like this by setting limits on screen time, social media, and other AI-driven platforms designed to capture endless engagement. These addictive behaviors are pulling kids away from real-world experiences, from creative play, and from each other.

But it's not just children who are vulnerable. She shared another concern about young adults forming deep emotional attachments to AI companions, virtual figures that remember their conversations, their struggles, their secrets. "Then one day," she said, "an update wipes out everything. And they're lost. Because the connection they thought they had was never real." I also have heard these stories. She went on to point out as risks to society the ways technology and AI are changing the way we relate to one another.

Something else to consider is the timeline for when Artificial General Intelligence (AGI) would be able to demonstrate human-level reasoning and problem-solving and no longer be confined to mundane tasks. Experts predict it could take decades to materialize, particularly considering the challenges to widespread adoption, ethical concerns, cybersecurity threats, regulatory frameworks, and unforeseen existential risks. As leaders, parents, and professionals navigating this uncertain future, we can only hope the focus will remain on wisely and responsibly guiding AI's development, to ensure it serves humanity rather than disrupts it, and works in tandem with emotional and social intelligence to allow meaningful human connection.

TAKE 11: FINDING EQUILIBRIUM: LETTING GO OF GUILT

Where do feelings of guilt come from? What is their root cause? The answer varies from person to person, and is not limited to any gender. It can stem from mindset, culture, and societal expectations. In some cultures, for example, working sixteen to seventeen hours a day is seen as a badge of honor, a source of pride and achievement. But at what cost?

The clients I've worked with who maintained these intense schedules for six to eighteen months often paid the price with their health. Some came down with severe colds or flu; others faced more dire consequences—a heart operation, a stroke that led to disability leave, and even complete burnout, requiring a full year off. Is it worth it? While labor laws exist to protect employees from over-work, many corporations prioritize bold goals over employee well-being. Some organizations claim to champion work-life balance, yet fail to walk the talk.

Guilt can also stem from systemic inequalities. Many female executives I've worked with pushed themselves beyond their limits, earned nonmonetary awards, and consistently exceeded expectations. Yet, their career advancement lagged behind their male counterparts, despite equal or superior performance. These women were justifiably frustrated, and often felt guilty about what their sacrifices had cost them—lost time with their families, missed time with their children and partners as well as friends and other family members.

Through coaching and self-reflection, these women uncovered patterns that fueled their guilt, including such things as holding themselves to impossibly high standards, taking on extra work, overworking due to pressure from senior leaders' high expectations, fearing that breaks or taking time off would be perceived as slacking, and equating long hours with pride and self-worth. It should be noted that these challenges are not exclusive to women; they resonate across genders, although they occur more frequently among women.

Overcoming guilt requires a deep exploration of its origins. This process, whether through root cause analysis, psychotherapy, coaching, or spiritual counseling, takes time and courage. It means confronting ingrained beliefs and gradually shifting behaviors. Having a support system can make all the difference while you're progressing forward with baby steps to make this change.

One client, a restaurant franchise owner, put this into practice. He told me, "I'm not going to tell my wife that I'm working on changing my guilt-driven work ethic. Instead, I'll focus on empowering my management team, delegating responsibilities, and truly embracing work-life balance. I'll know I've succeeded when she notices."

Four months later, he shared his success with a big grin: "My wife noticed. She appreciated that I was spending more time with her and the kids." She didn't ask him about the why, what, or how; she simply encouraged him to keep going. That moment validated his shift from overwork to balance, from guilt to joy. He now leads at the 30,000-foot level, with no regrets.

Guilt, whether stemming from cultural expectations, workplace pressures, or personal standards, can drive people to overwork at the expense of their well-being. Many high-achieving professionals, particularly women, face systemic barriers that add to this burden. The cost? Health issues, lost family time, and persistent guilt. Through self-reflection, coaching, and intentional change, individuals can break free from guilt's grip. The key is recognizing its root cause, shifting behaviors gradually, and surrounding yourself with a supportive network. As one client demonstrated, success isn't just about working less; it's about being fully present for what matters most.

TAKE 12: CHOOSING LOVE: IT'S TRANSFORMATIVE

Despite ongoing debates about diversity, equity, and inclusion (DEI), the National Football League (NFL) remains committed to supporting it. NFL Commissioner Roger Goodell has reiterated the league's dedication to it, including its efforts to interview minority candidates for coaching and executive positions.[23] For the past few years, the NFL has used the Super Bowl as a platform for messaging, displaying targeted slogans on the field beneath the goalposts. So, when the league replaced its previous slogan "End Racism" with "Choose Love," people took notice.

To my mind, this shift in messaging encourages a broader, more inclusive mindset that incorporates unconditional love as a guiding principle in addressing racism, discriminatory policies, and marginalized communities. It serves as a call to action. How can you integrate unconditional love into your approach to problem-solving, both personally and professionally?

It's heartening that companies like Apple, JPMorgan Chase, and Cisco continue to uphold their DEI initiatives and disheartening that iconic brands like Pepsi, Disney, and Walmart have chosen to remove references to diversity. In response to the fluctuating corporate landscape, I've advised Human

Resource (HR) executives in the DEI space to consider rebranding their teams with a title that aligns with their company's evolving perspective while preserving their core mission. Coincidentally, a client told me how, led by the CEO, her financial services institution changed their DEI terminology to "culture and core values" focused on their three core beliefs. HR had to change all written policies and communications as well as organize a road-show so all employees could become aware of the changes. By emphasizing diversity of thought, building team and organizational efficiencies, belonging, and a commitment to meritocracy and fairness, organizations can continue cultivating equitable opportunities for underrepresented groups, which is essential to countering both ingrained and unconscious biases. In my opinion, progress toward advancement is more important than perfection.

Beyond DEI, many organizations already embody the spirit of "Choose Love" by prioritizing well-being through Human Resources policies. International organizations, nongovernmental organizations (NGOs), and nonprofits extend their compassion to marginalized communities, including those caring for orphaned, injured, or endangered animals. Sustainability efforts are also on the rise, rooted in a love for our planet. Love, in its purest form, is a transformative force capable of reshaping the world.

A workplace culture built on love and empathy fosters trust and strengthens collaboration, leading to better outcomes. Research supports this. Companies with high-trust cultures experience 74 percent lower stress, 50 percent higher productivity, and 76 percent more engagement than those with low-trust environments.[24] Some forward-thinking companies are now incorporating empathy into performance reviews, recognizing that employees who uplift those around them drive exceptional results. If the NFL, a historically conservative organization, can publicly embrace a message of love, what's stopping today's business leaders from doing the same?

One Fortune 100 executive exemplifies this approach by aligning her leadership with her core value of being helpful. She actively supports new team members, guiding them through the company's culture and business dynamics, and clearly explaining the expectations for their roles. Months later, these employees express deep appreciation, reinforcing the fulfillment she finds in her work. Her leadership, rooted in love, empathy, service, and kindness, confirms the power of these so-called "soft skills," which experts argue are, in fact, the hardest to master.

Some skeptics argue that choosing love and building a high trust environment is impractical in high-pressure corporate environments, but Paul J. Zak, the author of *Trust Factor: The Science of Creating High-Performance Companies*, proved the opposite through his decades-long neuroscientific research.[25] Leaders who model love, trust, empathy, and kindness create workplaces where people find meaning and thrive. Zak's evidence corroborates that companies with empathetic leaders outperform their competitors in talent retention, innovation, and profitability.[26] A humancentric approach is good for business. When leaders model love, trust, empathy, and kindness, it sets a cultural standard, one that makes it uncomfortable for others to act in opposition to it. People, even introverts, are social animals, and they instinctively gravitate toward belonging, aligning themselves with the values that define their family, workplace, and society. Mindful leaders recognize this and make a choice.

They choose love.

So, how will you integrate love into your leadership? What would *choosing love* look like in your organization? In your family? In society?

TAKE 13: REWIRING YOURSELF: LIMITS AND POSSIBILITIES

When leaders want members of their team to develop their professional skills, they conduct the person's annual performance review and create a professional development plan for the following year; but, it turns out, most people don't change. This fact is the rationale for focusing on that team member's strengths and having other team members compensate for that person's weaknesses. Conversely, one senior executive in the food industry who benefited and grew due to a performance review and development plan told me, "I know I've succeeded when I have acquired a new set of skills to work on from my annual review. I'm grateful to my boss who guided me with that mindset." The process helped him focus on learning and growth with the knowledge that he had the capability to change and improve positively year over year.

Those who don't change eventually get pushed out of the organization, transferred to another team, and some remain in their role for years depending on the organization and industry. Sometimes it's for the best; however, sometimes it's for the worst, bloating the workforce and hurting morale on account of the inequitable distribution of work. The high performers tend to be given and take on more projects because they can get things done with excellence and on time. Although they're proud of their outstanding work ethic, they may feel the policy is unfair.

The low performers may have a strong work ethic but don't recognize that they are in the wrong position. They may even try to incrementally change, but their roles and responsibilities don't inspire them. They may be resistant to change because they are uncomfortable with unknowns or they may actually need that paycheck to support themselves, their families, or a sick father-in-law with expensive medical bills, and are afraid to jeopardize it by changing jobs. I've observed many leaders and humancentric organizations compassionately treat team members when health, mental well-being, and bereavement issues are at stake.

Can a low performer become an average or above average or even higher performer? I worked with a CEO in the energy sector who believed that anyone could grow through learning. He found that the most effective leaders were those who truly believed in their people, understood what motivated them both intrinsically and extrinsically, and pushed with them to achieve extraordinary results. It's a matter of time and investment and patience. You can set your team up for success. It reminds me of a Bollywood producer and director who also believed he could turn an unknown actor into a known one after his film reached box office success. The film succeeded and, indeed, the actor was recognized for his achievement. Additionally, I know of a college professor who believed in the capability of one of his students who was going through a difficult personal problem that interfered with his studies and gave him an A in his class. The professor's confidence in him motivated the student to continue on to get his master's degree instead of dropping out. These leaders were competent and confident and comfortable with bending the rules to help develop people in their spheres of influence.

You don't have to a be CEO, a movie producer, or a college professor to instill this belief system in your own team, division, or company. You can adapt this practice in your family life too. I often suggest that clients practice with their family members first, and then once refined, bring it the workplace.

Instead of leadership firing up to 20 percent of their workforce, then rehiring or hiring every year, it could be argued that more emphasis should be placed on cocreating positions best suited to people's talents, where they can contribute value and thrive. Building an environment where professionals are excited to go to work with renewed purpose and meaning as a result of their new roles and responsibilities is a benefit for the individual as well as the organization. This is true across industries.

Neuroscientists have discovered that the brain, when adapting to change, has the capacity to rewire itself through neural plasticity throughout life. Adaptation requires learning new skill sets, behaviors, and belief systems. To successfully adapt to the complex demands of the world, you have to overcome negative thought patterns, replace them with constructive ones, and consistently practice that mindset, which increases efficient communication between neurons, in effect, rewiring the brain for personal and professional development and advancement. Change and challenges test you to bring increased awareness and understanding to your limited knowledge, experience, and beliefs, and give you the choice to change. Resolving problems acts as a catalyst for you to learn new things and rewire your brain.

Although science supports the fact that people can change, humans are paradoxical. They develop blind spots and have unconscious biases and assumptions that play a role in keeping them resistant to change. Change starts with the desire for improvement or the highly important need to reduce either one's own or a loved one's anxiety. Self-improvement can be to desire to be a better communicator, or to follow a passion outside work, or to learn something new related to your profession.

One client, a robotics engineer, realized an urgent matter related to her tween-age son: urgent because she wanted to be the best mom ever and build a loving relationship with him. Whenever something happened, he would get angry and storm off. She, in turn, adopted a tough love approach; she would explain, try to solve her son's problems, and tell him to get over it and move on. Eventually, their relationship so deteriorated that they avoided one another. She came to me to work on her empathetic skills. We role-played scenarios that she later practiced with her son.

In the process, she realized that she also lacked empathy at work. Practicing at home would also help her become more empathetic in her professional relationships. Her husband, who was emotionally intelligent, also helped her. Often partners are complementary. The urgency she felt ignited the change within her to learn how to communicate with empathy in order to save her frozen relationship with her son. We explored where her assumption of tough love came from. It turned out that her father had treated her that way and she assumed that was the way to parent. Working together, she replaced tough love with empathic love. The change had a meaningful impact, which benefited both her family and colleagues, and she continues to practice her intentional, mindful, empathetic, and effective communication skills. Repetition and practice kept those neurons firing, and rewiring, leading to adaptive change.

Change relates to heart-brain coherence too. Thinking and acting tied to emotions, intuition, and feelings proves to be a powerful formula for developing and changing your mindset. Take "emotional ownership," a term the CEO of BlackRock, Larry Fink, uses. It involves the head and heart working together tied with action and accountability to responsible leadership. What stops some people from shifting their beliefs or transforming their mindset is sometimes linked to the person's inner critic to keep themself safe. Based on the context of your situation, ask yourself whether your need for self-preservation is a false assumption associated with outmoded beliefs. Taking time to reflect with a questioning mind helps you gain self-awareness. You'll be able to tap into your intuition or gut feeling and that will nudge you to take incremental action toward changing your habits and behaviors. As James Clear mentioned in his book *Atomic Habits*, "If you can get 1 percent better each day for one year, you'll end up 37 times better by the time you're done."[27] Focusing on incremental progress compounds results over time and repetition rewires the brain, building sustainable change in the areas of growth you intentionally develop.

Once you've rerouted your mindset within a safe and supportive environment with accountability partners, you'll notice that you see the world through a new lens or with fresh eyes. Things you once thought impossible become possible. Two clients I recall, one a CEO of a wealth management firm and the other a horse breeder, made the same comment: "I have to pinch my skin to know my life is real. I never dreamt I could achieve these turning points that transformed my life." Like so many people I know, you can tap into your innate courage and stretch yourself beyond your initial aspirations and dreams. When you engage in incremental change, you'll discover a new form of excitement and meaning in your life. You'll go beyond a survival mindset to a thriving mindset. You'll feel blessed and want to pay it forward to your family members, your friends, your colleagues, and those with whom you work and socialize. Combining all the elements mentioned, you can evolve and change while keeping your cherished values as your foundation.

Across my work with clients in Europe, the Middle East, India, China, Australia, New Zealand, and the Americas, I've uncovered some universal themes. It doesn't matter where you grew up, lived, or worked, you can still develop beliefs and mindsets that become outmoded over time. When you are aware of the hidden root causes that prevent you from changing, you are emboldened to embark on a path toward self-transformation, which takes effort, practice, iteration, persistence, patience, and self-compassion.

An "immunity to change road map" can help you identify the tension between the changes you aspire to make and the internal barriers holding you back.[28] For example, you might commit to uplifting your confidence by taking a visible seat at the table, trusting that senior leadership values your ideas and out-of-the-box perspectives. Yet, in practice, you might avoid speaking up in meetings, holding back your evidence-based insights or innovative thinking. This hesitation can stem from hidden competing commitments, for instance, not wanting to be perceived as an imposter or lacking expertise. Beneath those commitments often lie deep-seated assumptions that might have been shaped by past experiences, beliefs, or cultural norms, such as, "I'm shy," "I'm introverted," "I have social anxiety," or "In my culture, doing your job quietly is respected, while promoting your work is seen as boasting." By surfacing and testing these assumptions, you can begin to replace them with more empowering beliefs, enabling yourself to act with greater confidence, share your perspectives more freely, and ultimately create the positive change you seek.

This is a practical exercise you can use to map your own "immunity to change" X-ray.[29] Approach it as an experiment: choose a goal, surface the hidden commitments and assumptions that might be holding you back, and then test them in real life. Each time you gather evidence that an old belief doesn't hold up, you gain a reason to course-correct and step further into a new mindset. Over time, this practice aligns your thoughts and feelings, bringing greater alignment with heart-brain coherence. You can apply this not only for your personal growth but also with your team and organization, creating an ongoing cycle of reflection, testing, and transformation.

TAKE 14: NAVIGATING CONFLICT COLLABORATION:
A CATALYST FOR CHANGE

Conflict is inevitable in any setting—whether in the workplace, within families, or in broader society. It becomes a problem when leaders try to resolve it by telling others what to do without considering the other party's needs, which could range from speed of delivery to more money, from additional head count to handling heavy workloads to increased security, among many others.

Conflict, when viewed positively, can act as a catalyst for change; however, it needs to be managed. The way you approach conflict determines whether it becomes a destructive force or a growth opportunity. Skillful conflict collaboration is about moving beyond emotionally heated, adversarial standoffs—the "I'm right. You're wrong." approach—to building trust, strengthening relationships, finding common ground, solutioning together, turning tension into teamwork, and creating sustainable, win-win outcomes for all stakeholders.

At its core, skilled conflict collaboration requires a shift in mindset from winning to understanding, from defending to exploring, and from reacting to responding. It calls for emotional intelligence, social intelligence, active listening, empathy, problem-solving skills, mediation, and a structured approach to addressing disagreements with curiosity and openness rather than fear or avoidance. The best leaders navigate differences effectively, respect each person at the table, defuse shouting matches, ensure all point of views are fairly heard, guide conversations toward understanding, sometimes with the caveat of agreeing to disagree to reach resolution. Getting there may not come quickly or at the initial meeting. It may take a few meetings and require further feedback and iteration until it can be resolved thoughtfully. There are times when inflated egos are involved, in which case the best course of action based on intuitive decision-making is to walk away and accept the fact that you are not able to settle, compromise, or get to the win-win solution you wanted. In essence, you have to pick your battles.

Here is an example of a common conflict found in the workplace across sectors. One client, a VP of customer success, had to have a difficult conversation with her direct report, a senior customer success manager (CSM), who consistently paid no attention to details despite having been made aware of the issue. This situation required empathetic communication and the need to set clear expectations. Preparation was key. The VP gathered concrete examples of overlooked details and scheduled a one-to-one meeting for privacy. She asked clarifying questions to understand her report's perspective. She knew she had to listen respectfully and remain open, and that she then would seek collaboration on solutions so he'd be motivated to change his habits, take ownership of his tasks, and improve his performance.

During this one-on-one, the direct report pushed back and told her, "I've never been able to pay attention to details." She acknowledged his other strengths—he always exceeded his quarterly revenue targets and his ability to identify opportunities for his customers—but reminded him that his role and responsibilities included updating key account notes after customer calls in their Salesforce software versus keeping it in his head or on a private Excel sheet. The VP provided an example of a real-time issue that was the result of his negligence to document a customer issue with one of their products.

She explained her frustration and told him that his neglect to document his calls was affecting the team's workflow, decreasing efficiency in resolving problems, and diminishing customer trust. She took a deep breath and proceeded to ask him what he thought he could do differently. He reflected, then responded, "I'll schedule extra time on my calendar after customer calls and update the accounts so everyone knows where I stand."

The VP recognized his willingness to change and positively reinforced the lesson, saying, "This will help you stay organized and help the team address your customer issues, if you are unavailable." She continued, "What can I do to support you?" The CSM sat silently. She then said, "Let's have weekly instead of quarterly check-ins to ensure your progress in meeting your new goals." He agreed, and they worked out a schedule.

She noted to herself that during the weekly check-ins, she'd praise any improvements, knowing that positive reinforcement contributes to sustainable behavior change. In short, the objective of her conversation was not to reprimand her direct report but to clarify expectations and empower him to take ownership. She empathetically addressed the issue directly with the intention of skilled conflict collaboration to cocreate an action plan for improvement, act as his accountability partner, and coach him to embrace a growth mindset. Consistent one-on-ones and constructive feedback would help him achieve his short-term goals while professionally developing him toward his medium- and long-term aspirations, including an eventual promotion depending upon his performance exceeding expectations.

This VP through the coaching process utilized the communication framework to promote understanding by being curious and asking questions and staying open to his input. In a longer version, she could have paraphrased key points to ensure she understood him, but it wasn't necessary in this scenario. She also used the Nonviolent Communication (NVC): A Framework for Respectful Dialogue, developed by psychologist Marshall Rosenberg.[30] It's a process to help you express yourself authentically while listening to the needs of others emulating compassionate human behavior. This model can be used in personal and professional relationships, negotiations, and conflicts. The NVC process is broken down into four steps.[31]

1. **Observations (without judgment):** For example, "I've noticed examples of overlooked details." **(Use of "I" not "You"—"I" statements focus on the speaker's experiences and feelings. "You" statements can trigger defensiveness and arguments.)**
2. **Feelings (objective):** Don't take negative feedback personally and express yourself honestly. For example, "I feel frustrated because this is affecting the team's workflow and causing customer dissatisfaction."
3. **Needs:** Looking inward (managing from the inside out), the VP identified her feelings of frustration as well as the unmet needs of the team to provide timely answers to his customers when he was unavailable. This enabled her to be clear and make the following effective request.
4. **Requests:** Doable requests that enhance the requester's life and, in my example, the VP's ability to effectively lead her direct report's workflow and increase customer satisfaction.

Communication and NVC frameworks are designed to be adaptable, recognizing that every situation is unique and complex. Both emphasize an empathetic perspective and being conscious of each other's needs with the aim of creating mutual understanding leading to skillful conflict resolution. These approaches are invaluable for building personal and professional relationships, managing triggers and stressors, and handling challenging interactions with colleagues, clients, vendors, board members, activist investors, and diverse stakeholders across industries globally.

Improving communication skills is a universal theme that when adopted can create a more humancentric world based on the foundational values of dignity and respect. I encourage you to practice these useful techniques, take baby steps, reflect on your progress, iterate, and continue onwards. It is a lifelong process linked to taking care of yourself and others, reducing stress, enhancing well-being, and strengthening connections with compassionate intent.

APPLYING SKILLFUL CONFLICT COLLABORATION IN DAILY LIFE

- **At Home:** Approach family conflicts, in a psychologically safe space, with empathy, compassion, and unconditional love and a willingness to understand the underlying beliefs, thoughts, and emotions.
- **At Work:** Build a culture where disagreements drive creativity, innovation, and positive change rather than resistance, separation, division, disruption, and chaos.
- **In Society:** Engage in difficult conversations with the intent to find the middle path rather than cause rifts and disharmony.

When handled adeptly, conflict can build bridges, not walls, brick by brick. By embracing skillful conflict collaboration, you can construct environments where relationships thrive, teams innovate, and communities find solutions that benefit humanity.

TAKE 15: INFLUENCING WITHOUT AUTHORITY: LEVERAGE YOUR INNER ASSETS

Other than formal authority given by titles, there are ways to leverage your resources to lead others and bring them along with you toward achieving objectives. It begins by building trustworthy relationships. Taking the time to get to know your coworkers and key stakeholders can create allies when you treat others as human beings. When colleagues trust you, they're more inclined to follow you.

As a leader you need to acquire the ability to build strong relationships, collaborate with others, assemble teams to roll out initiatives across teams, divisions, and the organization. Humility proves important, as you can't do everything on your own; therefore, be humble—ask questions to receive answers. Everyone in the organization has a role to play, so be empathetic to diversity of thought; it helps you to learn and grow. Often, the people closest to the problem know the answer. If, as a leader, you are tasked with challenging the status quo, remember that people can rise to the occasion and solve problems; not everyone only sees constraints. Change involves risks: Asking people to stretch beyond their comfort zones, allowing them to make mistakes, reiterating with innovative thinking, and solutioning whether it concerns a reorganization or a customer's problem is essential. Trust, humility, and empathy are fundamental characteristics of relationship building, which is the foundation for effective leaders to influence without authority.

START WITH WHY

How do you make a case for change? A leadership expert, Simon Sinek, pointed out that when a leader leads with their "Why," it motivates people to take action.[32] Some clients have been coached to lead their teams with their Why and found it was an effective way to overcome resistance, build momentum to make progress, and achieve objectives in alignment with the organization's strategic plan to meet its goals. When you use this approach, you're creating a culture of values linked to belonging and purpose, rallying your team to achieve a collective goal, and helping your customers feel gratified.

For example, one leader turned around a team of software engineers, who had become demotivated because they only saw the details of what they were doing—primarily fixing bugs and implementing new features—without understanding how their work shaped the player experience for one of their popular games. The team leader noticed and asked marketing to find a fan-made video. At the next team meeting, he played the video showing a montage of streamers' heartfelt reactions to one game storyline; a father and son bonding over co-op play (cooperative play, where players work together toward a common goal); and players on forums sharing their experiences about how the game helped them in personal ways.

The leader addressed his team, "You're not just writing code. You're building worlds where people can escape, connect, learn from one another, and create memories. That bug fix you made yesterday made it possible for someone to have a meaningful experience. You're not just a bot doing a job. You are making the gaming experience great again. That's why you do this, that's why we're doing this together as a team."

A software engineer enthusiastically responded, now in alignment with their new Why, "Our UI improvement makes it easier for new players to get into the game."

The team leader replied, "Keep reframing your work. Think about how it relates to you and your positive impact on the gamer's experience."

By leading with Why, the leader reignited his team's passion for leveraging their technological skills to build games that deliver value through meaningful, engaging, and fun experiences driven by social connection, teamwork, and immersive problem-solving for the players. He was a transformative leader, inspiring his team with messages of belonging and purpose that emotionally resonated with them, and, therefore, they unconsciously became followers, influenced without authority, and, valuing their customers, they joined together to be of service.

Build-In Versus Buy-In

This concept came from my days working in public relations. It can be adapted to leadership through communications. Build-in refers to cultivating a resilient culture of trust, integrity, and credibility embedded in the organization's DNA. It's a long-term strategy that starts with thought leadership, storytelling, and internal alignment. Buy-in is more short-term focused and about persuading and getting support from key stakeholders and getting employees, customers, investors, or the public to agree on new initiatives or transformational change. Buy-in occurs through developing new messaging points, convincing teams, and creating trusted partnerships within the organization and its customers to align with new products and services. An effective influential strategy would combine both—build-in for long-term reputation building; buy-in for short-term persuasion.

A Fortune 100 healthcare products company, Johnson & Johnson (J&J) is often cited as purpose-driven, focused on research and development (R&D) and patient safety. In a *Times* interview, the CEO, Joaquin Duato, acknowledged the split from its consumer-health business that was the result of ongoing lawsuits related to its talc products that had been linked to ovarian cancer. He maintained both companies continued to value safety.[33] Under Duato's leadership, J&J shall continue to be purpose-driven, center its culture on trust and integrity, make decisions based on evidence, and ensure patient safety.

These values helped align employees internally with the company's values and its credo that was established by the founding family in 1943. Moreover, since 1886, J&J has been influential working with twenty-four US presidential administrations to advance healthcare.[34] Duato pointed out that employee engagement was high, over 90 percent, because they feel J&J is a principled company true to its credo.[35] This is an example of build-in, the long-term reputation-building strategy with key stakeholder resonance.

Duato, a servant leader and builder, wants to ensure J&J's continued growth long after his tenure. The biggest lesson that he learned and shared was, "Leadership, it's about people. It's about others. So leadership is not about the leader, but this is about a leader in how that individual can serve others."[36] In essence, leading with values, empathy, and integrity aligned with the company's mission, while continuously evolving, adapting, and innovating builds a sustainable, successful company lasting generations.

Being of service to others can be a form of influence without authority. Leadership is not one's title, position, or age. Anyone can be a leader. You can be leader when the occasion arises. It doesn't have to be all the time. It can be family, project, team, organization, or community based. Reflect on who your leadership role models are.

For Molly, it was her aunt Orin. A 2025 Oscar-winning short documentary *The Only Girl in the Orchestra* celebrates Orin O'Brian, a double bassist, the first woman to become a full-time member in the New York Philharmonic, a traditionally male-dominated field. Her niece, Molly O'Brian, directed this short film. Molly wanted to share the family story about her trailblazing aunt Orin, an exceptional artist, who humbly passed on her knowledge to future generations of musicians and was a leadership role model for Molly growing up. In the film, Orin reflected on her preference for playing a supportive role to her family, students, friends, and colleagues, in effect, being a servant leader. The film is a grand tribute to O'Brian contributing to classical music, opening doors for many female musicians, and inspiring members of her family.

NUDGES TO CHANGE BEHAVIOR

Based on how choices are presented, you can prod people to make decisions. This technique is often used in marketing, sales, behavioral economics, and policy-making, leveraging psychology with loss aversion, social norms, and pre-selected choices to make a decision easy for humans. Loss aversion exists as Fear of Missing Out (FOMO) on social media. When people follow others' behaviors, referred to as social proof, it helps them choose specific products and services. Some effective ways are through word of mouth as well as videos created by influencers that go viral, leading their followers to believe they must be part of the experience or suffer FOMO.

From a customer retention perspective, subscription models, like Amazon Prime's and Netflix's, make it easy for people to renew products or services. They don't have to think too much about it, as it's built-in to be automatically renewed, year after year, unless you opt out.

Another example is when HR leaders nudge employees into early retirement but give them freedom of choice. These tactics aim to benefit individuals, businesses, and society, but it's important to keep them ethically in check to avoid abuse of power.

Here's an example of the nudging technique used to effect positive change between two competitive team leaders, Michel and Jany, who were working on separate projects to solve the same problem. Both teams tapped into their teams' budgets and resources, doubling the cost and effort. When the division head brought it to their attention, they were reluctant to let go and merge their teams toward the common goal. The division head prepped in advance and showed them how working together would accelerate progress and reduce costs. She mentioned prior examples of successful collaborations to reinforce the idea that cooperation is an expected social norm within the company as one of its core values. She suggested that any savings that resulted from sharing their resources could be invested into future team-led initiatives, in this way nudging them by giving them freedom of choice, while emphasizing another corporate value of innovation through additional initiatives.

To get buy-in for the short-term scenario, she asked them how they could work better together. Michel and Jany proposed weekly meetings to stay aligned with the new objectives that would be communicated to their teams to build organic cross-team cooperation. The division lead's nudges helped

Michel and Jany motivate their teams toward this common project goal by integrating their resources, reducing redundancies, leveraging strengths, and overcoming their innate competitiveness in order to realign toward delivering an efficient solution that was in the best interest of everyone concerned—themselves, their teams, the division lead, senior leadership, and their customers. Nudging instead of forcing proves to be an effective tactic in leading and influencing others while *building-in* corporate values for enhanced persuasion and commitment. Subtly communicating the core values, she ensured her two leads remembered to make decisions in the company's best interests, simultaneously inspiring them to lead with purpose and feel proud of where they work.

EMPOWER OTHERS

Here's some wisdom from a former client, a FinTech COO, "Start with, you are meeting a new person every time you meet them." In other words, remain curious about the people you interact with as though you are learning something new about them each time. It's not unlike the Zen's beginner's mind philosophy, and is a means to understand the whole person. Human beings are complex, multidimensional, and contradictory. The objective of a human-centered society is to go beyond diversity, equity, inclusion, belonging, and justice toward treating everyone with respect and dignity—powerful core values that can start with the family, be practiced at work, and become a social norm globally. Respect and dignity when paired form a strong double bond, resulting in the stable O_2 molecule, the oxygen for a sustainable, compassionate, and just humanity. An aspiration worthy of striving toward, even if in increments of 1 percent improvement day over day. Knowing others helps you figure out what drives them so you can influence and empower them to be the best versions of themselves, whether at home, work, or in society.

Ariane, a VP of operations for a global tourism company, has been having trouble changing her unintentional micromanaging habit to one of empowering her team through motivation, inspiration, and belonging. She's committed to enabling world-class experiences for travelers but her hands-on, rolling up her sleeves and doing it herself approach has left her team feeling disempowered, leading to disengagement and quiet quitting.

During a coaching session, I asked her to provide context for a recent situation where she stepped in to resolve an issue rather than stepping back and letting her team take care of it. She mentioned how a high-end customer and his family missed a connection in Thailand on their flight to Japan. Her team, not accustomed to proactively taking charge, hesitated, but then alerted her to the problem. She resolved it successfully, reaching out to local vendors to rearrange logistics so the customer could be with his group on the next leg of the trip's itinerary.

I asked her to do a retrospective with her team to see how they felt about the way she handled this recent incident while it was fresh in everyone's minds. She reported back that her team felt grateful that she listened to their feedback; however, their feedback hurt her. They told her they were afraid to take over because of the way she micromanaged and appeared to do everything better. Ouch. I responded that it was understandable to want to uphold quality service but questioned her about how her team might be interpreting her management style on a deeper level. Like peeling away the layers of an onion, she was ready to reveal a hidden truth. Ariane looked down and recognized, "I'm not delegating because I don't trust them." Whoa!

Acknowledging the lack of trust and that we could explore that further in another session to get to the root cause, I suggested an action experiment in the form of a question: "How about letting go and empowering them to take ownership of their responsibilities with accountability so that you can focus on your own priorities?" She started singing the song "Let It Go" from Disney's *Frozen*. I smiled. When she finished, she asked, "How do I let go?" I told her how a client in the military explained that leadership can be "eyes on, hands off." She can oversee her team and let them figure things out. If they make mistakes, it's okay as long as they learn from them. They may even come up with better solutions. She would be creating an environment of ownership, learning to trust them incrementally, and helping them feel valued by giving them compliments and praise when merited. I reminded her she was changing a behavior, and it takes time, and to not beat herself up, have self-compassion, if she reverts to her old behavior. It starts with self-awareness, catching herself, then practicing her new habits with baby steps until it becomes unconscious and natural, successfully rewiring the brain. At first, it takes work and effort, but it pays off and her entourage will notice it and let her know.

Ariane committed to shifting her leadership style from micromanagement to one of empowerment by building a high-performing culture where motivation, inspiration, and belonging became the core values. Over time, this increased her team's engagement and success while giving her more space to focus on high-level strategy. This type of challenge is prevalent across industries worldwide, no matter your title or position. Delegating, believing in your team, trusting your colleagues while holding them accountable comprise other elements of influence without authority.

Influence without authority is about producing results through collaboration rather than coercion, especially in complex, global environments. Effective leaders create influence through the dual strategy of build-in and buy-in, aligning shared interests through credibility, trust, and mutual benefit. They nudge behavior change by incrementally transforming environments, setting expectations, and modeling desired actions, rather than relying solely on directives. True influence comes from empowering others, not just by motivating them with praise and recognition, but by inspiring them through vision, core values, purpose, and a sense of belonging. For leaders, mastering this approach means cultivating relationships, understanding individual and cultural differences, and leveraging emotional intelligence to guide others toward meaningful, lasting change.

You can be the North Star shining your light on others. In leadership, this means you can provide guidance, clarity, and inspiration to those around you. Just as the North Star has historically helped travelers navigate their journey, a strong leader shines a steady light, offering direction in times of uncertainty. This kind of leadership isn't about controlling others but rather subtle influence without authority. You're illuminating pathways so people can find their own way with confidence. By leading with integrity, vision, values, authenticity, and consistency, you become a reliable point of reference, empowering those around you to grow and succeed. When you shine your light, you give others the courage to shine theirs. Everyone has something of value to contribute.

TAKE 16: PLAYING THE GAME: INCREASE VISIBILITY AND WORKPLACE POLITICS

In any professional environment, technical expertise alone is not enough to advance your career. Increasing visibility and navigating workplace politics are essential skills for executive presence, influence, and long-term success. Many professionals shy away from these aspects, viewing them as manipulative, not part of their culture, or simply unnecessary. However, when approached with integrity, strategic visibility, and political acumen, they can help you along your leadership pathway while you're contributing business value and financial impact to your organization.

Part of the challenge is figuring out the unspoken rules of the game. Every workplace has a power structure, decision-making dynamics, and informal networks that influence whether you are going to get recognized or not, depending on whether you're willing to play the game. When you learn and understand these unspoken rules, you'll be better positioned to advocate for yourself, show how your team has grown, create innovative products and services, and increase revenue in alignment with the company's goals. The first step toward playing the game effectively is recognizing that visibility and politics are part of the process. It's neither good nor bad.

Referring back to shifting beliefs and mindsets, you can reframe what visibility means to you. Some clients don't like self-promotion or boasting because of the way they were brought up; the countries they lived in and their inherent social norms; or perhaps they're shy, introverted, and prefer to remain in the background. However, if you reframe increasing visibility and executive presence as adding value based on your experience, expertise, ideas, and contributions and let key leaders know about your competence, they'll notice. Often executives recognize high performance, but in a very competitive world, it's better to build strategic relationships and communicate your impact with humility, not bragging. In this manner, the key stakeholders will notice you and reward you.

One client in the hedge fund world was adept at soft politics. He was up for promotion and intentional about building strong relationships across the firm, engaging his leaders, getting known for his work, and communicating his team's impact that contributed substantially to the bottom line. He told me it felt like he was networking around 80 percent of his time and working 20 percent. That's the first time I heard those stats and felt he was exaggerating, as he was known as a star performer. I related this story to another client, who was reticent about increasing his visibility, but reversed the metric—20 percent networking and 80 percent devoted to their role, while going above and beyond responsibilities to demonstrate leadership capabilities. He did get his promotion through hard work and being comfortable playing the game.

By contrast, I've seen a few clients miss out on promotions because they assumed their work spoke for itself. When they saw their peers advancing, it frustrated them. Exceeding expectations isn't enough, whether you're working remotely or in hybrid fashion. I asked one of them, "What have you observed that your peer did differently?" She replied, "She gave presentations at company workshops showing how she built a team from twenty to four hundred in five years, expanding from one country to fifteen, increasing their scope of products and services, and crediting her team with innovative-ness, taking ownership, being accountable, and collaborating across teams regionally—in effect, becoming the highest revenue generator for the com-pany." After this revealing conversation, we cocreated a strategy to enhance her self-advocacy skills and to stretch her beyond her comfort zone to be a participant versus a spectator in the game of organizational politics.

Some practical strategies to increase your visibility begin with building your reputation. Share how you want others to perceive you beyond your role and responsibilities. You can, first, communicate your achievements and your team's milestones during a relevant group workshop, forum, or town hall demonstrating your leadership, business, and strategic acumen. At a team retrospective, you can discuss lessons learned and insights gained.

Second, build strategic relationships with key decision-makers, senior leaders, and peers across teams who discuss your contributions when you're not present. Consistently engage with your network and make it genuine. Offer to be of service to them when needed so it eventually becomes a fair exchange of give and take.

Third, speak up at meetings. Introverts and shy clients have a difficult time contributing to discussions until they realize they're adding value, a fresh perspective, and expertise that perhaps no one at the meeting has with their depth. Don't speak just to be seen as some boisterous people do because they think that's how to get noticed—they get noticed but get pigeon-holed as annoying. Better to add insight, ask a thoughtful question, or nod your head in agreement to show support—it's more genuine.

Fourth, leverage public platforms in-house and externally at conferences showcasing your expertise or thought leadership, activities that expand your influence to a wider audience. Fifth, advocate for others by supporting and elevating them—for example, as a division head, highlight the achievements of your team leaders. This helps you build high-trust performing teams, enhance visibility of colleagues, and create a network of mutual, beneficial impact.

It's a best practice to navigate workplace politics with integrity—not duplicity, toxicity, or whiplash. Relationships, influence, and decision-making compose the core elements of politics. Ethical political acumen means understanding power structures, aligning with key objectives, and influencing outcomes while staying true to your primary values. As a leader, you can authentically position yourself as a trusted voice within your organization while tactically engaging in politics.

Visibility and politics are not about playing a game of deception. It's about making sure that your contributions are recognized and that you have a seat at the table where decisions are made. Many people want a seat at the table. By practicing these skills with competence, confidence, and integrity while strategizing three moves ahead like a chess player, you can enhance your leadership impact and create lasting influence in your organization. If you don't play the game, someone else will make up the rules for you. Step up, stand out, and lead with intentional purpose.

TAKE 17: PLAYING THE GAME DIFFERENTLY: RETHINKING RULES FOR SUCCESS

During coaching conversations, sometimes the film *Moneyball* comes up. It's a movie adapted from Michael Lewis's book *Moneyball: The Art of Winning an Unfair Game* and based on true events.[37] General manager for the Oakland As baseball team Billy Bean challenged traditional scouting wisdom, adopting a new approach, sabermetrics, to recruit baseball players. Sabermetrics uses data and statistics to determine the effectiveness of a player; notably, "the total of a player's on-base percentage and his slugging average," not the number of home runs.[38] If you dig deeper, this concept comes from Bill James's book *1977 Baseball Abstract: Featuring 18 Categories of Statistical Information That You Just Can't Find Anywhere Else.*[39] In essence, sabermetrics revolutionized the baseball industry, built winning teams, and has since been applied at different companies across industries.

This approach comes up when clients feel stuck with the same-old, same-old. I ask what could they create to energize them? Some think deeply and say, "It's not about hitting a homerun. It's about getting to first base." What smaller projects can they work on, align on goals with another department, to create a new feature, product, or service that gets them to first base? They keep building upon these small hits until they have solid traction and demonstrable success and then go on to create a big project to work on with their dream team. It works. True, it's a baseball metaphor used by fans because of the film's popularity, but it has become mainstream when applied to organizations.

At times, I draw upon my entrepreneurial and seed investor background and coach entrepreneurs and senior executives who are either starting up new companies based on their passion or as an exit plan from their day jobs at corporate, government, or international organizations. Utilizing leadership tactics from *Moneyball*, I coached a client, Chaplain Karim, around creating his dream startup. I love to encourage people to follow their dreams and feel fulfilled, especially when they integrate a holistic perspective that includes quality time for self-care, family, friends, and societal endeavors beyond work. It's a doable venture.

I devised three principles from the *Moneyball* paradigm that I suggest clients incorporate when thinking about creating a new product or service or business, but there may be more. It starts out as a brainstorming session. We are co-thought partners.

The following example is not literal, but it reflects the essence of the process. The first principle we used from *Moneyball* was about challenging conventional wisdom. Chaplain Karim was a Lebanese Christian living in the States. Chaplains are spiritual professionals who provide religious guidance and counseling in secular settings like hospitals, hospices, cruise ships, and the military. They're highly valued in the communities they serve. He was planning his exit strategy. Once he retired, he dreamt of having a food truck combining faith, food, and community. We had fun cocreating his vision for faith and food on the move. It wasn't only about serving fresh, organic food with a Middle Eastern flair, but also feeding the soul, bringing faith and guidance through conversations, to communities he'd be traveling to across America. At each location, there would be a space for gathering and storytelling, reconnecting with a higher wisdom in a down-to-earth, nonjudgmental way. He wanted to include all religions, even atheists and agnostics, therefore his food truck would be known as *The Ministry of Common Sense*.

Incorporating the second principle, he would make AI and data-driven decisions. For his social purpose venture, research questions included how to fund his food truck, find his target audience, and find relevant locations. His criteria for data-driven insights would center on cities with faith-based community events, local churches and nonprofits that he could partner with to offer mobile faith-based gatherings with nourishment, weekend markets, food truck festivals, music festivals, along with an emphasis on fresh, organic farm-to-table food offerings highlighting flavors from the Middle East. With this data, he would be able to plan a cost-effective, high-impact travel route, and focus on smaller cities where his mission could connect with people. He made one exception: to attend one big food festival per year.

In terms of success metrics, Chaplain Karim knew it was based on sales and revenues per location, but he decided to redefine success metrics as the number of meaningful conversations per stop, not profits. I asked if this was realistic.

Principle three concerned turning constraints into strengths. He told me how his operation would be volunteer heavy, have multiple sources of income; it would be subscription based, use crowdfunding like Classy, Mightycause, or Donorbox, find sponsors with socially responsible food brands, create merchandise with inspirational messages sold at the truck and online, and eventually, write a cookbook featuring recipes served on the truck, paired with spiritual reflections. There was much more detail, but he definitely had been thinking in detail about creating his faith-based food truck ministry.

Maybe we were naïve, but we felt there would be no real resistance to change, although people might joke that a food truck wasn't a church or place to gather around and have meaningful spiritual conversations. Chaplain Karim hoped his customers would stay and engage in discussions where they needed guidance during these times of constant change and uncertainty. His overarching vision, his *Ministry of Common Sense* food truck, would be more than a business; it would be a faith-based movement based on his values of being of service and social connection. His mission would be to plant a seed—one meal, one conversation, and one act of compassion at a time, until it bloomed into group gatherings where faith and food could travel together.

Utilizing these three adapted principles from *Moneyball* with a focus on data and metrics would form the foundation for how Chaplain Karim would build his mobile ministry, not by throwing spaghetti noodles at a wall and seeing which ones would stick, or building a plane in the air, which I have seen other startups do, but by balancing food sales, donations, and community partners through a bona fide strategy. May his dream come true where every meal, gathering, and act of generosity energizes the next steps on his journey.

I have used this as a case study you can follow, whether you're an entrepreneur or an executive in an organization ready to branch out on your own to create meaningful impact in whatever area excites you.

TAKE 18: LISTENING TO YOUR HEART: A TWENTY-ONE-DAY EXPERIMENT IN TRUTH

World number one tennis player Aryna Sabalenka spoke after winning her match against British Sonay Kartak at the 2025 Indian Wells tennis tournament.[40] She emphasized focusing on self-improvement and treating people as human beings. The interviewer cited her kind gesture of stopping her warm-up to take a picture with a mother and child. Aryna has become a beloved figure in her spheres of influence for living a balanced life and interacting with others with respect and dignity from heart-centered leadership.

The day Sabalenka won her match to go into the quarterfinals at Indian Wells, I came across an article I wrote seven years ago titled *What Is True*

Versus What Is Truth? As someone who has spent decades exploring self-help, personal growth, and professional development, I often use myself as a testing ground for new ideas. One experiment stood out: For twenty-one days, the time often cited as necessary to shift a habit or adopt a new perspective, I committed to a simple practice: Every morning, I placed my hand over my heart and asked, *"What would you like me to know today?"* Throughout the day, I remained mindful of the message, and, in the evening, I reflected: *Was it true? Or did it contain a deeper Truth?* The goal was to discern whether my heart consciousness aka intuition or soul was speaking or if it was merely my ego. Here are some of the most profound insights I attained from this journey. Here is a sample of my daily reflections:

DAY 2: GO FORTH WITH LOVE

That morning's message was clear: *Go forth with love.* It immediately brought my late grandmother to mind. She had spent countless hours volunteering with New York's City Meals on Wheels. In her honor, I decided to donate 90 percent of the royalties from my book *Mindful Communications* to this nonprofit. Love, I realized, is more than an emotion; it's an action intertwined with meaningful purpose giving you a sense of significance in life.

DAY 3: SELF-COMPASSION

My inner critic was relentless that day, berating me for a business venture that flopped. Curiously, the message I received that morning—*self-compassion*—urged me to respond differently. As I allowed myself to feel the heavy emotions of my own negative self-judgment, tears streamed down my cheeks. From accepting my mistakes and learning from them came the release of outmoded beliefs, attitudes, and behaviors. The new thought turned to *I get to* create a more positive growth mindset. There is no absolute right or wrong, only perceptions and interpretations that form our behavior within the context of the situation, influenced by circumstances, relationships, decisions, and consequences. Tolerance, understanding, and self-compassion are essential for self-leadership and leadership of others.

DAY 9: STEADY PROGRESS:
IT'S ABOUT THE JOURNEY

Patience has never been my strong suit, but that morning's message reminded me: *It's about the journey, not the destination.* The idea of steady progress resonated deeply. Life isn't about rushing to an outcome; it's about being present with what unfolds. We are both the creators and the observers of our own stories. Somewhere along the way, I had encountered the question: *What's true versus what is Truth?* True is what the ego perceives; Truth is what the heart consciousness or soul knows.

DAY 12: REST IS PART OF THE PROCESS

As a multipotentialite, I often feel the need to be in constant motion. But that day, my heart whispered, *It's okay to pause. Rest. Rejuvenate.* I saw it clearly: Downtime isn't wasted time. It prepares us for the moments when life accelerates, so we meet them with energy rather than exhaustion.

DAY 16: THE COMBAT OVER JOY

That morning, my heart's message was simple: *Joy!* My ego scoffed: *Joy? You've got to be kidding. When was the last time you truly felt joy?* But my heart pushed back: *I allow myself to receive joy today.*

I decided to let the day unfold and see what happened. By evening, I had experienced an unexpected visit from a dear friend, an inspiring conversation with a successful tech CEO, and news that my family would be gathering for my upcoming visit—something rare and meaningful. None of these moments were grand, yet each carried profound joy. The heart had spoken Truth.

DAY 21: TRUST YOUR INTUITION

It felt like the perfect closing note to this experiment. Over the twenty-one days, I had practiced tuning in, listening, and discerning. Each morning, I asked. Each day, I stayed open. Each night, I reflected. And in doing so, I strengthened my ability to recognize when my heart consciousness was speaking—when Truth, not just what seemed true, was being revealed.

AN INVITATION TO LISTEN

This simple experiment takes only a few minutes in the morning, a check-in during the day, and a moment of reflection in the evening. Yet, its impact can be profound. If you're curious, try it yourself. It deepens your self-awareness, a foundational quality for effective leadership for yourself and others. Commit to twenty-one days of consciously listening to your heart and see what unfolds. By being present and engaged, you may discover that the Truth has been trying to speak to you all along.

Hello, can you hear me?

A PARTING LETTER: TO A LIFELONG EXPEDITION

With deep appreciation and an open heart,
I send my gratitude flowing toward you,
for your time, your curiosity, and your presence here.
May your path be rich with insight,
your discoveries bold with truth.
Let's keep the conversation alive.
I'd love to hear where your journey takes you.
With love, respect, and warmth

—Laura Thompson

ACKNOWLEDGMENTS

It's always about the journey. This one began after a three-month sojourn in Hawaii, where I achieved the long-held goal of finishing my novel. I returned to the mainland and stayed with a dear friend in Palos Verdes Estates, California, to attend a literary conference in Los Angeles with the intention of submitting my novel to a literary agent.

Over coffee one morning, a conversation with my friend sparked a new idea: What if I wrote a leadership book? She challenged me to sketch out an outline. Suddenly, I had two books to pitch. I owe the genesis of this book to that moment and to Tracy Nickl, PhD, a friendship that dates back to our days at Simmons University. The novel, for now, was placed on the back burner.

At the conference, I met Eric Lincoln Miller, who believed in my leadership book and became my literary agent. Together with Deanna Brady, we crafted the nonfiction book proposal. Included were two early endorsements: one from Mitzi Perdue and the other from Captain David Gallimore. I'm especially grateful to Mitzi, who has long supported my professional journey and exemplifies compassionate leadership. I'm equally honored to have Captain Gallimore's backing.

Thanks to Eric's persistence, I eventually met editors Laurie Harting and Phil Marino along with Airié Stuart, publisher at Church Publishing Incorporated. A contract was signed. As often happens, change followed. Though I didn't end up working with Laurie and Phil directly, I remain thankful for their support in moving the project forward. I also appreciate Eric's relentless determination from A to Z and, of course, his renegade personality that kept things interesting along the way.

I was fortunate to work with Roma Maitlall, who stepped in as associate editor and immediately saw the big picture. She brought all the puzzle pieces together, elevating the manuscript's clarity, cohesion, and impact. Roma has been a joy to work with and was collaborative, responsive, and remarkably steady throughout the process.

I also want to thank Brianna Lopez, Ellen Coleman, Tania Bissell, and Amy Wagner for their collective hard work on production editing, developmental editing, line editing, copyediting, and proofreading. A special thanks to Ellen for spotting paradoxes and nudging me to include further examples to clarify meaning for the reader as her suggestions proved invaluable.

Endorsements were another important part of this journey. Mitzi introduced me to Mark Victor Hansen. I've long admired his work, especially his commitment to honoring people's unique and uplifting stories. It's not unlike coaching—helping others become the best versions of themselves. I'm deeply grateful to Mark for his generous and inspiring endorsement.

Since 2021, I've had the pleasure of knowing Samuel H. Kim, founding president of the Center for Asia Leadership. From the start, he has encouraged my work, and we've collaborated on a range of coaching and teaching projects through his organization in the Asia-Pacific region. Working with Samuel and his team has been a joy. He's been a guiding light, and I hope we continue to partner to create meaningful, values-based change in communities and organizations around the world.

That spirit of collaboration has also been at the heart of my own journey. This book couldn't have been written without the coaching, mentoring, and advising relationships I've had the privilege of building over the past decade. Every client has been important to me. Our symbiotic connections allowed us both to grow, and for that, I'm deeply grateful. Thank you for being part of my life.

Finally, my unconditional love and deep appreciation flow to my family and friends near and far who have walked beside me on this journey of life, and to the colleagues, mentors, and fellow travelers whose wisdom, encouragement, and quiet acts of kindness have left a lasting mark along the way.

NOTES

CHAPTER ONE

1. EEngagement, "Towers & Watson: Employee Engagement Statistics," The Employee Engagement Group, 2022, https://employeeengagement.com/towers-watson-employee-engagement-statistics.
2. "Branded," vol. 3, *Break Free from Plastic Brand Audit 2020*, https://www.breakfreefromplastic.org/wp-content/uploads/2020/12/BFFP-2020-Brand-Audit-Report.pdf.
3. "Self-actualization" is a term originally coined by German psychiatrist Kurt Goldstein and was popularized by Abraham Maslow, an American psychologist, who included the term at the apex of his hierarchy of needs.

CHAPTER TWO

1. "Tech Optimists from Google Use AI to Reach Development Goals," United Nations, UN Interviews, June 7, 2024, https://news.un.org/en/audio/2024/06/1150771.
2. Thich Nhat Hanh, *The Art of Communicating* (HarperOne, 2013).
3. Daniel Goleman, *Emotional Intelligence: Why It Can Matter More Than IQ* (Bantam Books, 1995). The term was coined in 1990 by Peter Salovey and John D. Mayer, whom Goleman credits as having "invented the whole field."
4. Richard Barrett, *Evolutionary Coaching, A Values-Based Approach to Unleashing Human Potential* (Lulu Publishing Services, 2014), 182.
5. Barrett, *Evolutionary Coaching*, 182.
6. The phrase "reptilian brain" was coined by Paul D. MacLean, a neuroscientist, as applied to brain development. The theory is no longer widely accepted. I and others find it a useful metaphor.
7. This phrase is thought to have been coined by H. Igor Ansoff, author of *Corporate Strategy: An Analytic Approach to Business Policy for Growth and Expansion* (McGraw-Hill, 1965).
8. Kendra Cherry, "What Is Empathy?: How It Helps Strengthen Our Relationships," Verywell Mind, updated July 3, 2024, https://www.verywellmind.com/what-is-empathy-2795562.

9. Stephen R. Covey, *The 7 Habits of Highly Effective People: Powerful Lessons in Personal Change* (Free Press, 1989), 43.

CHAPTER THREE

1. People with high D scores in the DISC assessment are described as competitive, confident, and independent, and sometimes can be perceived as forceful or controlling. They communicate directly without softening their tone, unless learned. This can sometimes lead to difficult conversations when conversing with those who prefer a collaborative and indirect style of communication.
2. Benjamin Huff, *The Tao of Pooh* (Penguin Books, 1983).

CHAPTER FOUR

1. Sheldon Reid, "What It Means to Be Neurodivergent," HelpGuide.org, updated April 11, 2025, https://www.helpguide.org/mental-health/wellbeing/being-neurodivergent.
2. According to Jonathan Hancock, the technique was invented by Sakichi Toyoda, the founder of Toyota Industries in the 1930s. It was popularized in the 1970s, and Toyota still uses it. Jonathan Hancock, "5 Whys: Getting to the Root of a Problem Quickly," Mindtools, last modified June 30, 2025, https://www.mindtools.com/a3mi00v/5-whys.

CHAPTER FIVE

1. Jenna Garden, "Patagonia CEO: A Force for Environmental Change," Stanford Business, April 21, 2020, https://www.gsb.stanford.edu/insights/patagonia-ceo-force-environmental-change.
2. Commonly attributed to Maya Angelou, though no verified source confirms her authorship. The quote predates her usage and is attributed to Carl W. Buehner in 1971. The original quote is from Carl W. Buehner, in *Richard Evans' Quote Book* (Publishers Press, 1971), 244, col. 2: "They may forget what you said—but they never forget how you made them feel."
3. Travel and Leisure Staff, "47 Dalai Lama Quotes That Will Change the Way You See the World," *Travel and Leisure*, updated May 23, 2024, https://www.travelandleisure.com/travel-tips/celebrity-travel/dalai-lama-quotes-travel-inspiration.
4. *Young India* was a weekly journal and a series of books published by Mahatma Gandhi from 1919 to 1931. The journal was a platform for Gandhi to spread his ideas on nonviolence and India's independence from British rule. The book *Young India* is a collection of his articles from the weekly journal, originally published in two volumes, one covering 1919–1922, the other 1924–1926.

This quote is attributed to Mahatma Gandhi and is not specifically from a single edition of *Young India* but rather is a widely recognized saying associated with his philosophy on self-discovery through selfless service. It appears in various writings and speeches throughout his career, including in the publication *Young India*.

5. Howard Schultz and Dori Jones Yang, *Pour Your Heart into It: How Starbucks Built a Company One Cup at a Time* (Hyperion, 1997).

6. Andrew Tonner, "9 Indra Nooyi Quotes on Leadership, Diversity, and Business That Will Make You a Better Investor," The Motley Fool, updated October 26, 2018, https://www.fool.com/investing/2016/11/19/9-indra-nooyi-quotes-on-leadership-diversity-and-b.aspx.

7. The Investopedia Team, "Understanding Intrapreneurs: Their Role, History, and Company Benefits," Investopedia, updated September 25, 2025, https://www.investopedia.com/terms/i/intrapreneur.asp.

8. Lauren Bernal, "I'm with the Brand," Medium, March 12, 2019, https://medium.com/zendesk-creative-blog/im-with-the-brand-7b64038430c8.

CHAPTER SIX

1. Sundar Pichai, "A diverse mix of voices leads to better discussions, decisions, and outcomes for everyone," quoted in Sharon Florentine, "Still Asking Why Tech Struggles with Diversity and Inclusion? Google It," *CIO*, September 22, 2017, https://www.cio.com/article/230700/still-asking-why-tech-struggles-with-diversity-and-inclusion-google-it.html.

2. Andrew St. George, "Leadership Lessons from the Royal Navy," McKinsey and Company, January 1, 2013, https://www.mckinsey.com/capabilities/people-and-organizational-performance/our-insights/leadership-lessons-from-the-royal-navy#/.

CHAPTER SEVEN

1. Kenneth H. Blanchard, *Leading at a Higher Level: Blanchard on Leadership and Creating High-Performing Organizations*, 2nd ed. (Pearson/FT Press, 2009), 276.

2. See https://keirsey.com/assessments/products-temperament-workplace/#to-scroll-product. If you wish to learn more about the assessment and its subcategories, visit this site or ask someone in Human Resources at your organization for this tool.

CHAPTER EIGHT

1. Michael Mink, "Strategic Planning Need Not Be a Dreaded Annual Chore," *Investor's Business Daily*, December 20, 2024, https://www.investors.com/news/management/leaders-and-success/strategic-planning-need-not-be-a-dreaded-annual-chore/.

2. Marina Gorbis, "Five Principles for Thinking Like a Futurist," *Educause Review* (Winter 2019), https://er.educause.edu/articles/2019/3/five -principles-for-thinking-like-a-futurist.

3. "How Many Star Trek Fans Are There?," The SciFi Reel, YouTube, March 7, 2025, https://www.youtube.com/watch?v=NQuI6TAxWPE.

4. You can learn more about their scenario thinking skills at https: //www.shell.com/news-and-insights/scenarios.html#vanity -aHR0cHM6Ly93d3cuc2hlbGwuY29tL3NjZW5hcmlvcy5odG1s.

5. "What Are Shell Scenarios?" Shell, https://www.shell.com/news-and-insights /scenarios/what-are-shell-scenarios.html, accessed March 7, 2025.

6. Interview with Angela Wilkinson by Larisa Tatge, "Scenario Planning: An Insider's View," *IESE Insight* 12 (2012): 42–43.

7. A score that measures the average percentage of trust in institutions, Edelman Trust Barometer, https://www.edelman.com/trust/trust-barometer.

8. Benjamin Larsen and Virginia Dignum, "AI Value Alignment: How We Can Align Artificial Intelligence with Human Values," World Economic Forum, October 17, 2024, https://www.weforum.org/stories/2024/10/ai-value-alignment -how-we-can-align-artificial-intelligence-with-human-values/.

9. Larsen and Dignum, "AI Value Alignment."

10. Larsen and Dignum, "AI Value Alignment."

11. Marko Perisic, "The Powerful Impact of AI on Workplace Behaviour and Wellbeing," *theHRDirector*, February 4, 2025, https://www.thehrdirector.com /business-news/ai/powerful-impact-ai-workplace-behaviour-wellbeing/.

12. Jacqueline Carter, Rasmus Hougaard, Marissa Afton, and Katharina Kassubeck, "Using AI to Make You a More Compassionate Leader," *Harvard Business Review*, February 18, 2025, https://hbr.org/2025/02/using-ai-to-make-you-a-more -compassionate-leader.

13. "Bob Iger Teaches Business Strategy and Leadership," MasterClass, 2021, https:// www.masterclass.com/classes/bob-iger-teaches-business-strategy-and-leadership.

CHAPTER NINE

1. Albert Einstein, "The Real Problem Is in the Hearts of Men," *The New York Times*, June 23, 1946, https://www.nytimes.com/1946/06/23/archives/the-real -problem-is-in-the-hearts-of-men-professor-einstein-says-a.html. His thoughts, insights, and wisdom pertaining to humanity, creativity, and leadership are just as relevant and powerful today as they were when he lived.

2. Jonathan Derbyshire, "Year in a Word: Polycrisis," *Financial Times*, January 1, 2023, https://www.ft.com/content/f6c4f63c-aa71-46f0-a0a7-c2a4c4a3c0f1. Polycrisis, as a term, appears to have been first used in the 1990s by French social scientists Edgar Morin and Anne Brigitte Hern to describe the "interwoven and overlapping crises" facing humanity, particularly in the ecological realm.

3. The term "Intelligence Age" is thought to have been coined by Sam Altman, CEO of OpenAI. The term "antifragility" was coined by Nassim Nicholas Taleb, a risk engineer and quantitative analyst, and author of the book *Antifragile* (Random House, 2012). "Antifragile" is the ability to become more robust when exposed to stressors, uncertainty, or risk, according to dictionary.com.

4. Nassim Nicholas Taleb, *Antifragile: Things That Gain from Disorder*, repr. (Random House, 2014). Mr. Taleb is considered one of the foremost thinkers of our time, and this book reveals how to thrive in an uncertain world.

5. Raj Dharmaraj, "Thriving in Chaos: The Power of Antifragility in Leadership and Organizations," Effilor Consulting, August 27, 2024, https://www.effilor.com/post/thriving-in-chaos-the-power-of-antifragility-in-leadership-and-organizations.

6. Kasia Broussalian talks to Heba Saleh and Patricia Nilsson, "Volkswagen's Dire Warning," *Financial Times*, September 5, 2024, https://www.ft.com/content/6ec3e973-108c-474a-bff5-0c9b37da924c.

7. Henry Adobor, "How Organizations Can Benefit from Volatility: The Promise of Antifragility and Some Cautionary Notes," *Organizational Dynamics* 54, no. 1 (March 2025): 101098, https://doi.org/10.1016/j.orgdyn.2024.101098.

8. Carsten Krause, "Case Study: Amazon's AI-Driven Supply Chain: A Blueprint for the Future of Global Logistics," *The CDO Times*, August 22, 2024, https://cdotimes.com/2024/08/23/case-study-amazons-ai-driven-supply-chain-a-blueprint-for-the-future-of-global-logistics/.

9. Krause, "Case Study."

10. Krause, "Case Study."

11. Krause, "Case Study."

12. Irene Herrera, "Building on Tradition—1,400 Years of a Family Business," *Works That Work*, no. 3 (2014), https://worksthatwork.com/3/kongo-gumi.

13. Herrera, "Building on Tradition."

14. Peter M. Senge, *The Fifth Discipline: The Art & Practice of the Learning Organization* (Doubleday/Currency, 1990), chap. 9–12.

15. Senge, *Fifth Discipline*, 14.

16. Adobor, "How Organizations Can Benefit from Volatility."

17. Adobor, "How Organizations Can Benefit from Volatility," 7.

18. Adobor, "How Organizations Can Benefit from Volatility," 5.

CHAPTER ELEVEN

1. Jim Baker, "The Story of Three Bricklayers—A Parable About the Power of Purpose," Sacred Structures, April 9, 2019, https://sacredstructures.org/mission/the-story-of-three-bricklayers-a-parable-about-the-power-of-purpose/.

2. Martin Luther King Jr., Barratt Junior High School, October 26, 1967. This quote appears in his speech to students addressing the theme of dignity in labor and excellence in one's calling.

CHAPTER TWELVE

1. "Nearly 80 Reproductive Health, Rights, and Justice Organizations Unveil Proactive Blueprint for Sexual and Reproductive Health, Rights, and Justice," Planned Parenthood Press Release, July 15, 2019, https://www.planned parenthood.org/about-us/newsroom/press-releases/nearly-80-reproductive-health -rights-and-justice-organizations-unveil-proactive-blueprint-for-sexual-and -reproductive-health-rights-and-justice.

2. Aidan McCullen, "Organisational Stress Wood: Struggle Builds Resilience," *The Innovation Show*, June 30, 2022, https://theinnovationshow.io/organisational -stress-wood-struggle-builds-resilience/.

3. Tim Tebow Foundation home page, https://www.timtebowfoundation.org.

4. Night to Shine: Tebow's Special Needs Ministry, https://www.specialstrong.com /night-to-shine-tebows-special-needs-ministry.

5. Erik Van Alstine, *Automatic Influence: New Power for Change in Work and Life* (Stone Lounge Press, 2016). "Intending good" refers to acting with sincere benevolent intent, guiding others toward positive outcomes and transformations while respecting their autonomy.

6. Dr. Andleeb Asghar, "The Science of Self-Love: The Evidence-Based Benefits of Loving Yourself," Ness Labs, 2022, https://nesslabs.com/self-love.

7. Office of Communications, "The Benefits of Self-Forgiveness," Stanford Medicine News Center, August 2, 2019, https://scopeblog.stanford.edu/2019/08 /02/the-benefits-of-self-forgiveness/.

8. Daniel S. Lobel, "People-Pleasing as a Symptom of Childhood Trauma," *Psychology Today*, August 4, 2024, https://www.psychologytoday.com/us/blog/my-side-of-the -couch/202408/people-pleasing-as-a-symptom-of-childhood-trauma.

9. Oxford Languages, https://www.google.com/search?q=define+imposter +syndrome&rlz=1C1UEAD_.

10. John Rau, "What's Up with CEO 'Imposter Syndrome'? Here's the Truth," *Forbes*, July 25, 2024, https://www.forbes.com/sites/johnrau/2024/07/25/whats -up-with-ceo-imposter-syndrome-heres-the-truth. This data is based on a recent Korn Ferry Survey entitled "Workforce 2024 Global Insights Report."

11. Rau, "What's Up with CEO 'Imposter Syndrome'?"

12. Kara Baskin, "New Research Debunks 4 Myths about 'Impostor Syndrome,'" MIT Management Sloan School, January 13, 2025, https://mitsloan.mit.edu/ideas -made-to-matter/new-research-debunks-4-myths-about-impostor-syndrome.

13. Baskin, "New Research Debunks 4 Myths about 'Impostor Syndrome.'"

14. "Feeling Like a Fraud? A Deep Dive into Impostor Syndrome," Mass General Brigham McLean, January 21, 2025, https://www.mcleanhospital.org/essential /impostor-syndrome.

15. Matthew Klint, "Doug Parker, CEO of American Airlines, Offers Career Advice," *Live and Let's Fly*, November 7, 2019, https://liveandletsfly.com/doug -parker-career-advice.

16. Andre Agassi, *Open* (Alfred A Knopf, 2009), 365.

17. Lauren Landry, "Why Emotional Intelligence Is Important in Leadership," Harvard Business School Online, April 3, 2019, updated June 11, 2024, https://online.hbs.edu/blog/post/emotional-intelligence-in-leadership.

18. Psychologist Edward Thorndike first coined the term "social intelligence" in 1920, describing it as the ability to "understand and manage men and women, boys and girls—to act wisely in human relations." See Dara Rossi, "Highly Effective Leaders Have High Social Intelligence," Workplace Peace Institute, September 5, 2024, https://www.workplacepeaceinstitute.com/post/highly-effective-leaders-have-high-social-intelligence.

19. Maggie Sass, "What a High Emotional Intelligence Looks Like," TalentSmartEQ, August 11, 2025, https://www.talentsmarteq.com/what-a-high-emotional-intelligence-looks-like/. Original chart model courtesy of Travis Bradberry.

20. Sass, "What a High Emotional Intelligence Looks Like." Original chart model courtesy of Travis Bradberry.

21. GTD, "Better EQ, Better Performance," TalentSmartEQ, December 15, 2020, https://www.talentsmarteq.com/emotional-intelligence-at-workplace-to-improve-performance/.

22. Sass, "What a High Emotional Intelligence Looks Like." Original chart model courtesy of Travis Bradberry.

23. Cassandra Cassidy, "NFL Replaces 'End Racism' with 'Choose Love,'" Morning Brew, February 6, 2025, https://www.morningbrew.com/stories/2025/02/06/nfl-replaces-end-racism-with-choose-love.

24. Paul J. Zak, "The Neuroscience of Trust: Management Behaviors That Foster Employee Engagement," *Harvard Business Review*, January–February 2017, https://hbr.org/2017/01/the-neuroscience-of-trust.

25. Zak, "Neuroscience of Trust."

26. Zak, "Neuroscience of Trust."

27. James Clear, *Atomic Habits: An Easy & Proven Way to Build Good Habits & Break Bad Ones* (Avery, 2018), 15.

28. Robert Kegan and Lisa Laskow Lahey, *Immunity to Change: How to Overcome It and Unlock the Potential in Yourself and Your Organization* (Harvard Business Review Press, 2009), 231.

29. Kegan and Lahey, *Immunity to Change*, 249.

30. Joshua Schultz, "Your Complete Nonviolent Communication Guide," *Positive Communication* (blog), October 1, 2020, https://positivepsychology.com/non-violent-communication/.

31. Schultz, "Your Complete Nonviolent Communication Guide."

32. Simon Sinek, *Start with Why: How Great Leaders Inspire Everyone to Take Action* (Portfolio, 2009).

33. Ayesha Javed, "Why Johnson & Johnson's CEO Welcomes Scrutiny," *Time*, February 3, 2025, https://time.com/7212011/joaquin-duato-johnson-and-johnson-interview/.

34. Javed, "Why Johnson & Johnson's CEO Welcomes Scrutiny."

35. Javed, "Why Johnson & Johnson's CEO Welcomes Scrutiny."

36. Javed, "Why Johnson & Johnson's CEO Welcomes Scrutiny."
37. Michael Lewis, *Moneyball: The Art of Winning an Unfair Game* (W. W. Norton & Company, 2003).
38. Robin Powell, "What Investors Can Learn from Moneyball," TEBI, December 3, 2024, https://www.evidenceinvestor.com/post/what-investors-can-learn-from-moneyball.
39. Powell, "What Investors Can Learn from Moneyball."
40. BNP Paribas Open, "Aryna Sabalenka—March 12, 2025: Press Conference (A. Sabalenka/S. Kartal 6-1, 6-2)," BNP Paribas Open, March 12, 2025, press conference transcript, https://bnpparibasopen.com/news/aryna-sabalenka-march-12-2025.

INDEX

ABOUT THE AUTHOR

Laura Thompson, MA, PCC, is an executive leadership and communications coach, author, and thought leader with over a decade of experience guiding senior leaders across industries worldwide. A sought-after speaker and member of both the Harvard Business Review Advisory Council and the Fortune AIQ Advisory Board, she brings a global perspective and twenty-five years of expertise spanning entrepreneurship, finance, and communications. Laura empowers leaders to drive purposeful transformation within themselves, their organizations, and society through strategic insight, emotional intelligence, and authentic human connection. She holds an MA in international relations and international political economy from Boston University (France), a BA in finance from Simmons University, and has also studied at INSEAD Business School. An American expat for half her life and a devoted Francophile, Laura brings curiosity, warmth, and deep cultural sensitivity to everything she does.